BE BRAVE

What does it mean to be brave?

Bravery isn't about being fearless—far from it. Instead, bravery is when you recognize that you are afraid, but you do it anyway. Because when you are scared you have two options: you can use it as an excuse to give up, or you can grab hold of your courage, and face your fears.

And that's where we, the editors of *Teen Breathe*, can help. Every month we read the latest research on what it takes to be confident in who you are, so that you're able to say what you really think, and do those things that scare you. And now we're excited to pass that knowledge on to you.

So next time you worry that you don't fit in, find yourself facing a sticky friendship situation, or are frightened to try something new, this is the book for you. We hope it will prove that you can do it, it's good to stand out, and you are unique—and that's what makes you awesome.

Be brave and free

CONTENTS

DO YOU BELIEVE?

Do you feel able to take on the world? Believing in yourself gives you enthusiasm for life, an inner confidence, a sense of what is right, and, most importantly, a feeling that anything is possible

Do you believe in yourself? Do you feel sure of your strengths and abilities? Not in an arrogant, "I'm so amazing" way, but in an honest one that means you know who you are and accept every part of yourself—the good and the bad. Because believing in yourself can be harder than you might think. If you believe that you are capable of whatever life throws at you, you feel more ready for life's experiences. You know you can rely on your strengths and abilities to handle everyday challenges, and you are likely to embrace opportunities rather than shy away from them. And even when things don't go as planned, your belief in yourself can help you to try again. When you're faced with a task that you find difficult, you think "I can," or "With practice I can," rather than "I can't."

Accepting the good
Has anyone ever told you that you're funny? That you're kind, or creative? Good at sports, at writing, or that you work hard? Did you believe them when they said those things? When those around you notice your strengths and talents, it can give your confidence a boost—but only if you believe what they've said is actually true. Is that voice inside you friendly, encouraging you to accept it when someone says something nice about you? Or is it harsh and mean, making you doubt what they say? If so, then that's the opposite of believing in yourself.

Learning to believe
The best way to nurture the belief that you can do it, is through using the abilities that you have, learning and practicing and, importantly, trying again when things don't work out. The more you do, the more you'll discover and see what you're truly capable of. When you focus on what you *can* do, you start to take pride in your achievements, and then your belief becomes even stronger.

BUILD YOUR SELF-BELIEF

There are some other things you can do to boost your confidence…

1 Choose friends wisely
Surround yourself with people who make you feel good. A lot of how you see yourself is based on how you think other people see you. Don't waste your time with people who aren't positive, and don't get too bogged down by approval and reactions on social media.

2 Don't compare yourself to others
Everyone has their own strengths and weaknesses, and yours will be different to your friends'. Embrace everything about yourself, quirks and all, and you won't be wishing you were more like somebody else.

3 Be kind to yourself
When your inner voice is mean or negative, stop and say something positive instead. If it says, "I can't," say "I can." If it says, "I'll never be able to do it," say, "With some hard work I can learn how to do this."

4 Take some risks
Try new things, say yes when opportunities come up, try out for a team, raise your hand in class more often, say what you really think (as long as it won't hurt someone's feelings!).

5 Be true to yourself
It takes courage to be the real you. The more honest you are about who you are, to yourself and to others, the more you will believe in yourself. Feel confident in your actions and don't worry that you need to act a certain way to fit in with others. Don't be embarrassed about wanting to do your best and never feel foolish for trying. Let others see you for who you are—mistakes, insecurities, the lot. When you don't feel you have to hide something you can't do well, suddenly it doesn't seem as important.

VISUALIZATION

Believe in yourself and discover anything is possible

When facing a challenge or dealing with an unfamiliar situation, you may not always believe you're talented or smart enough to achieve a successful outcome. Whatever your goal, though, it's important to start with the right attitude and believe in yourself, and visualization—or mental imagery—is a great way to boost your confidence.

Visualization is about mentally taking yourself through a future event and seeing a successful outcome. If you want to win a game of tennis, or perform well in a school debate, focus and imagine yourself lifting that trophy or being congratulated by friends and teachers. Keep envisioning success over and over in your mind, and you begin to believe it will happen.

Scientifically proven to improve self-esteem and performance, many professional athletes, including Olympic rower Steve Redgrave and basketball player Michael Jordan, have been known to use the technique as a tool to help them feel confident before competitions. And media success story Oprah Winfrey credits visualization and positive thinking with helping her to pull herself out of poverty and go on to become one of the wealthiest women in the world. As a child she watched her grandmother working her fingers to the bone and determined her life would be better. She said on *The Oprah Winfrey Show*: "Create the highest, grandest vision possible for your life, because you become what you believe."

SEEING IS BELIEVING

Envision your success and you'll start to feel you really can do it…

1 Be the star, not the audience
Find a comfortable and quiet place to relax, where you won't be interrupted. Close your eyes, take a few deep breaths, and give yourself some time to settle down and calm your mind. Now visualize yourself getting ready for the event. Be sure to imagine this from your own perspective. Try not to watch yourself as if you're in a movie.

2 Make a stand
Picture the place where you're about to perform the activity in your mind. This may be the running track, the stage, or the classroom. See yourself standing with a strong, confident posture, or visualize yourself walking toward the situation with your head up. Then, run through the entire event as you would wish it to happen, from start to finish.

3 Turn on all of your senses
Visualization doesn't just have to focus on the visual—in fact, the more senses you can engage, the more successful the technique is likely to be. What do you smell, hear, or feel? Immerse yourself as fully in the mental image as you can—it should feel as though it is actually happening. It should be so detailed that it takes as long to picture it as it would to do it in real life.

4 Practice makes perfect
This isn't about wishful thinking, or simply picturing your success. It's about mentally practicing the activity you want to do well, and actually seeing that the outcome you're after is possible. The more you can practice the technique, the better you'll get at it.

Am I WEIRD?

Why it's normal to feel strange as you try to figure
out who you are and where you fit in

So, you've been invited to a party but you'd prefer to stay at home. Finally, at the last minute, you decide to go. You stand there, the only one who doesn't seem keen on tasting the suspicious-looking drink. You're half-listening to the crowd, finding it all pretty boring. You've made an effort and tried to mingle, but nothing will do. Today, more than ever, you're convinced you're socially awkward, out of place. Does this mean you're weird?

The beauty of difference

Firstly, while you might be feeling misunderstood, lonely, or lost, it doesn't make you weird. Secondly, weird isn't bad—it's different. Finally, have you considered you might be comparing yourself to the "wrong" people?

The fact that you enjoy staying at home suggests you're happy with your own company. This is good, not weird. You don't want to drink alcohol? A-OK. You're not interested in the subjects of conversation? Ditto. It might be that you're with people who just aren't your crowd.

So, you're out of place, perhaps, but not necessarily socially awkward. You're not like the other people around you at that particular moment in that environment at that time. That's fine. Everyone's unique—it's what makes the world beautiful. Being different is, in fact, normal. Knowing who you really are, however, can be more complicated.

WHAT MAKES YOU
DIFFERENT
OR
WEIRD
THAT'S YOUR
STRENGTH

Meryl Streep

Embrace your uniqueness

Younger children are often told how special they are, but the meaning of this word changes as you get older and start comparing yourself to other students. Sometimes it can seem to highlight how different you are and challenge your identity instead of celebrating your uniqueness.

It creates doubts and raises one question in particular: who am I? Answers don't come easily. It takes time and experience to find out who you truly are, and one of the best ways to learn how "to be" is by observing the people around you. But by doing so, you also worry more about what they're thinking about you. It's a natural instinct to try to find your own group and to want to be accepted by them. To *be* like them, even.

The thing is, this applies to everyone. Even the most popular student at school wasn't born self-assured. In the quest to blend in, it can sometimes be hard to see differences as advantages.

We don't all have to be the same

Have you ever thought your quirkiness could be a real strength? Some of the world's most influential thinkers and scientists, among them Albert Einstein, were called weird when they were young. Others were bullied for daring to be different (it was apparently her school bullies that gave Taylor Swift the inspiration to start writing songs).

You might be criticized and teased for many reasons, sometimes for none at all. This could be because others feel insecure, are threatened, and don't understand you. Why? It might be because you don't fit into their idea of the norm—but that's all right. The world doesn't need everyone to be the same, it needs more diversity, more individuals. Fresh ideas, new visions, and a different way of thinking all help to spark creative originality.

In short, it's okay to feel weird. The important thing is to love and embrace your differences—and carry on being weird. You never know where it will lead you…

Ways to join in and remain true to yourself

* Accept yourself the way you are
* Resist peer pressure
* Find people who are similar to you
* Respect the unique qualities of others
* Be open to doing and learning new things
* Try to belong rather than fit in

LEARNING TO FLY

Are you struggling at school? Everyone has something they find difficult, but if you can ask for help where it's needed and remember to celebrate your strengths, things will get easier

If you're struggling with your learning at school, whether it's with math, staying focused, writing, or reading, you might see yourself as less clever than others. You might even have a diagnosis of a learning difficulty like dyslexia or ADHD, and see it as a handicap or illness, wishing it away so you can be "normal" and more like your friends. That's what many people who find things hard at school think—it's natural to want to be as good as your peers at everything. But what if you really were top of the class at everything you tried? Wouldn't you stop being you? The way you learn is part of who you are—it's about a whole way of being. You can't just wish away the difficult stuff. It's important to understand all the qualities that make you who you are, not just to focus on what you can't do.

Looking for what makes you special and different is at least as important. The difficulties you might have are like a price tag attached to a whole set of talents. Make it your mission to look for those gifts. They don't always show up at school. The actor Orlando Bloom is not the first celebrity to say that his dyslexia was the thing that inspired him to overcome obstacles and achieve.

"Wanting to be someone else is a waste of the person you are"

Marilyn Monroe

BUILD YOUR CONFIDENCE

* Get to know yourself better. Listen carefully to the compliments you get and try to feel and accept their truth. Maybe draw a tree or flower and every time you realize a talent, skill, or character trait, or discover which things or causes matter to you, write them on a branch or petal. Use a large piece of paper, colorful pens, and perhaps pin it to your wall so that you see the drawing develop over time.

* Being self-critical and having doubts is part of the game. You will also have critics or negative people around you who are quick to fire off nasty comments or poke fun. As you know, trying to ignore them doesn't always work. Every day I still put out a few chairs in the chamber of my mind for those (inner and outer) critics. I tell them I know that they are there, but I'm doing my things anyway.

* Know your real friends and be in touch with them as often as you can. Know too, how much you are loved and by whom.

* Learn to be alone and even disconnected from social media for some periods at a time. Creative people throughout history have known how important it is to temporarily remove yourself from the world. Then you can put the best of yourself back into it.

* Be relaxed about making mistakes and accept setbacks as part of life. But look for the rainbow in your clouds. Find something to learn from these situations.

TIPS FOR LEARNING

* Listen to lots of audiobooks. Maybe read along as you listen. Stories are vital for your emotional development. Don't let your reading level stop you from getting the best that literature has to offer as a way to understand life.

* When reading, try to translate words into a movie in your head. This will also help you remember things better.

* When you're writing, start by focusing only on the content. Picture what you want to say in your head, get it all down on paper without worrying about spelling or punctuation, and only when it's all there in front of you should you go back to the grammar. Don't let fears about writing perfectly stop you from expressing yourself.

And finally…

* Learn breathing techniques to stay calm or try meditation, there are lots of good guides online.

* Your sleep is important, get as much as you can.

* Don't believe anything written here, try everything out for yourself and see if it works!

SHAKE UP
YOUR THINKING

Have you ever heard the expression "think outside the box"? This phrase is often used when new and original solutions are required, rather than the usual ideas that commonly spring to mind. But why do most people tend to think in the same way, and can you learn to think more creatively?

If you got together a group of people and asked them to solve a problem—such as, "How could we raise funds for a local charity this year?"—the likelihood is that most of them will give similar answers. Their thoughts will immediately turn to their previous experiences and they'll use their existing knowledge of the world. Few will come up with truly unique or innovative solutions.

While learning from the past is often helpful, there are times when it's good to think in bold new ways. The world's greatest scientists, innovators, artists, writers, and entrepreneurs all have one thing in common—the ability to think creatively. Whatever their field of expertise, successful people realize if they continue to do things as they've been done before, they'll continue to get the same results.

Opening your mind

People who think outside the box take the same information as everybody else but look at it differently. Creative thinkers ask questions. For example, when chemist Spencer Silver failed to create an adhesive strong enough for use in aircraft, instead of discarding it, he asked: "Well, what could this be used for?" And ta-dah!—with his weak glue, he created the world's very first sticky notes in 1974.

Imagine you're on the school's environmental committee. For three years, assemblies and various posters about reusing and recycling have failed to make any real difference to the amount of waste left after lunch. How about every student makes their own reusable food wrap in shop class? The more diverse ideas you can generate, the more likely you are to find one that works.

HOW TO BE MORE CREATIVE

Learning to think outside the box helps you to solve problems, respond to changing circumstances, and cope with new challenges. Here are some ways to train your brain to view things differently:

1 **Find an object in your environment (for example, a paper clip, pebble, book, mug, or glass jar). How many different uses can you think of for this object?**
Example: *Uses for an empty jar: A drinking vessel, a vase, a tea-light holder, a time capsule, food storage, a display "cabinet" for small objects, a desk organizer, a spider catcher, or a plant container.*

2 **Consider how you could complete a task without using one of the usual tools, ingredients, or methods**
Examples: *How could you paint a picture without a paintbrush? How could you wash your hair if you couldn't lift your arms above shoulder height? How could you put your socks on without using your hands?*

3 **Play a game of Taboo™ with friends. Players have to describe a word without using that word or five related words. Other team members must guess the word**
Examples: *Describe the word "tennis" without saying the word "tennis" or the words: court, racket, tennis ball, net, and US Open. Describe the word "jeans" without saying the word "jeans" or the words: denim, blue, pants, clothing, and wear.*

4 **Choose two seemingly unrelated objects and see if you can find a link**
Examples: *Squirrel/pencil. Link: Squirrels live in trees and pencils are made from wood. Stapler/trampoline. Link: Both contain springs.*

Keep on learning to improve your ability to make new connections, and ask as many questions as you can about the world around you.

A FRESH START

Whether it's a new school, new college, or new job, a fresh start often equals a mixture of excitement and apprehension. But what do you do if it feels overwhelming?

Make no mistake about it, moving up from elementary to high school, high school to college, or even changing classes mid-year is a significant step. It can be difficult finding your way around a fresh set of maze-like corridors, getting to grips with a complicated timetable, and weighing up what the teachers are like—and that's to say nothing of having to meet lots of new people.

It's even tougher if you're the only one among your elementary-school friends who's going to your new high school and you can't check with your best friend that you're heading in the right direction for the gym hall.

Even so, don't panic. Instead, be prepared. There are three areas where good prepping could work wonders—read on to find out more about them, and pick up some top tips for making new friends at the same time.

1 Feeling unprepared

Start organizing yourself, your equipment, and your clothes ahead of the start date. If, for instance, your new class demands specific books or equipment that can only be bought online, order them well in advance so there's no last-minute "out-of-stock" scenario.

A few days before, think about what you might wear and how you wish to present yourself. It's a good idea to make sure your outfit is clean, pressed, and ready the evening before it's needed, too. We'll return to this later, but for now let's just say no one wants to be panicking about what to wear 10 minutes before they're due to leave the house.

Another night-before job is to double-check you have everything you're going to need. This can help you to feel reassured on your way in and also makes it less likely that you'll end up freaking out when you suddenly realize you don't have your pencil case, a main textbook, or, worse, lunch money.

If you want to be sure everything's in place you could even make your lunch the night before and put it in the refrigerator—that way, all you have to do in the morning is wash, get dressed, eat breakfast, and head out. No last-minute worries.

2 Navigating your way around a new building

It can feel embarrassing when you're unsure of where everything is and no one wants to get lost on the way to class. Many schools have a handy map of the buildings near the reception desk. But if you still have trouble, just ask someone—

people will be happy to help. It's just a matter of plucking up the courage to talk to an older student or teacher who looks like they know their way around and asking them for directions. Once you've got the hang of speaking to people you don't know, this isn't such a big step, and you'll soon be getting around with no trouble at all.

3 First impressions

It doesn't matter what age you are, first impressions count. So before your first day, it might be an idea to have a mini-pamper session to ensure you're feeling as fresh as a daisy when you walk through the school or college doors. Maybe you could wash your hair and trim your nails to make sure you look neat, presentable, and approachable. The important thing is to feel comfortable in your own skin as this will help you to feel reassured among your new peers. If you think you're not looking your best—or you're wearing clothes that aren't really you—your confidence might dip and you'll be more likely to clam up. So, be yourself, avoid last-minute panics, and put your best foot forward.

MAKING NEW FRIENDS

When you start somewhere new it's always handy to have someone there that you know, however this isn't always possible if you've moved away or gone to a completely different school than all your friends. If you're starting high school or college the first thing you should know is this—it's okay to feel nervous. Everyone is. It may sound like friends and family are just saying this to make you feel better but, honestly, it's totally true.

So now, with this in mind you can understand that everyone is in the same situation and everyone is probably looking for some solace, so just keep calm and breathe. When you're ready, here are a few suggestions on how you can approach people and begin to boost your confidence:

* **Strike up a conversation** Maybe try to chat with someone by complimenting them on their bag or pencil case, or if you're in college, something that they're wearing.

* **Ask a question** Try asking a question to keep the conversation going, for example: "So, which elementary school did you go to?" or "I love that top/dress/jacket on you! Where did you get it?"

* **Find common ground** If the answer to your previous question was somewhere you also like to shop, you already have something in common. You can talk about your own experiences and purchases there. If not, ask a question you think might be relevant to them. For example, if they're reading a book, you could ask what it's about and whether they have a favorite author. Or, if they're wearing a band T-shirt and seem to be into music, ask the name of their top band. Their answers could lead to book and song recommendations and shared interests.

* **Join a club** It may sound obvious, but signing up for extracurricular activities in which you're interested will increase the likelihood of meeting like-minded students, especially ones who might not be in your class.

* **Smile!** It's an instant way of looking more approachable and making other students feel comfortable enough to ask you questions. And the more people you meet, the more likely you are to make new friends and build a broader social circle.

Friendships take time

The main thing is not to worry and not to try too hard. Some students feel they must find a group of friends or a best friend immediately or else they'll be lonely and miserable the whole time. This isn't the case. It can take several weeks before a real friendship starts to form, so don't panic if you don't click with someone instantly. If you have trouble finding good friends after a couple of months, don't blame yourself. It could be the school or college that's the issue (not all schools suit every type of person), so don't be afraid to ask your family for a change if you feel it's necessary.

GETTING YOUR VOICE HEARD

How to make people in authority listen to you

Are you one of those people who has lots of ideas but sometimes feels frustrated because no one seems to listen? Or, are you too shy or nervous to voice your opinions because you feel you won't be taken seriously, particularly if it's to someone who's in a position of authority? If so, now's the time to take action. Your viewpoints and ideas are important and with a little help, you can learn to get your voice heard by people with power, whether it's speaking to your principal about updating school rules or talking to your local government about improving facilities for young people in your area.

HOW TO GET YOUR IDEAS HEARD AND CONSIDERED

1 Get involved

Most schools and colleges have a council and most involve campaigning and voting in order to be a member. So, if you're keen on making a difference and have good ideas, join it. Don't worry if you're not elected or too late to join this year—speak to current members or the leader of the council about how you can get involved as they are your representatives, after all, and always need help.

2 Write it down

If something concerns you or you have a good idea but are too nervous about saying these in person, write a letter so you can get all your ideas down in a polite, constructive, and balanced way. Be positive, nonjudgmental, and, where appropriate, offer solutions. You can write it or type it, you may even email it if that feels appropriate, but spend time planning it first. What points do you want to get across? What do you want to achieve? Which person do you want to read this?

3 Gather your evidence

Back up your arguments and ideas with facts. It could be you do a survey of other students to see what they feel or that you spend a few weeks making notes about a situation. It may be a personal story that will give your ideas more weight. For example, if the sandwiches in the school cafeteria have the same fillings three weeks in a row, show a list. If you think there's a need for a change in your town, explain why.

4 Be polite and persuasive

Good manners, honesty, politeness, and respect for others' viewpoints will stand you in good stead whether you discuss your ideas in person or by letter. It's also important to stay calm and not to tell the person in authority that they're wrong. For example, if your issue is with cafeteria food, don't just say it's all disgusting—give details about what could be improved and ideas for getting more students to buy the food. Describe the ways a situation could be made better for the benefit of many people.

5 Phrases to use
When trying to get your point across, it's a good idea to have a few stock phrases in your head to use. You should aim to show that you understand the other person's point of view but then illustrate to them why your idea is better.

For example:
* I understand that you believe... however...
* While I realize it is important to... many students feel...
* I appreciate you taking the time to hear my argument about...
* Could you advise me where to go next with my ideas?
* What steps do you recommend I take next in order to change this?

6 Remember the person you're speaking to is human too
The person you talk to or write to may be in a position of power, but they were a student once, too, and should listen to you whether or not they can help. Just speak to them with maturity and good manners and they will respond to you. You may not get the answer you want, but taking the time to try will boost your confidence for when you have to raise another issue in future.

7 Join a club
If you're particularly interested in something,  join a club or association dedicated to your cause. For example, it may have to do with changing the environment, recycling plastic, sexuality, or animal rights. And if you can't find one, start one up with the permission of your principal and parents. Being with other people who have the same opinions will only strengthen your arguments. Another good way of improving your argumentative and persuasive skills is joining your school's debate club. Who knows—your ideas may lead to changes you want.

8 Don't take things personally
When you've got your ideas across, you may be successful and see positive changes as a result. However, it may be that despite your best efforts, the person you speak to won't listen or does listen but can't or won't change anything. Take time to reflect on the decision. You can come back to the issue but you may need to spend some time considering how else to get your ideas across—or whether the situation has to be accepted for now. Equally, if things aren't happening as fast you'd like them to, recognize that things may only happen gradually at first, but small changes you instigate could have a big impact.

TAKE THREE
FRIENDS...

What to do when a group of
three suddenly feels more
like two plus one

"Two's company, three's a crowd" is one of the best-known sayings in the English language and one that many people, young and old, have experienced personally—and painfully.

While having two best friends and being in a tight-knit trio should spell double the fun and double the intimacy, the reality is often different. The dynamic of a threesome can be tricky—even toxic—as it's inevitable that sooner or later, someone will feel sidelined. It may never be as brutal as two against one, but it might appear as if it's two and one: A duo with a singleton tagging along behind. Being the singleton can cause a lot of heartache—you may feel isolated and rejected by your friends and become a little resentful, particularly if you're the reason your other two friends know each other. It's never going to be easy seeing people who were your friends first and foremost forming a close bond that seems to exclude you.

If you've ever been in a trio, you may recognize this scenario: There you are in your band of three—you're so close that even your teachers joke that you're joined at the hip, and call you the three musketeers. But then you find out that your two best friends, the two people you thought you could trust with your life, have been meeting up after school without you. There are posts about what they've been doing all over Instagram™, and looking at the photos of them

together at the movies, and enjoying a girls' night in at one of their houses afterward, makes you feel betrayed.

You may want to confront them, to ask them why they left you out, but you worry that would only bring them closer together, so instead you post a message, just to let them know that you know what they've been up to. You say something like "that looks like fun," when inside you're screaming "why didn't you invite me? I hate both of you right now."

It's perfectly normal to feel like this, and perfectly normal, too, if you find that you don't want to see your friends. You may want to stay at home to lick your wounds, even though you know that wouldn't help anyone, least of all you. What would be best would be to speak to your friends, particularly if something similar has happened before. If it's just an isolated incident, you could try to ignore it, and focus on the positive aspects of your friendship—how much you like both of them—and how good your relationship is or, better still, take the initiative and plan something for the three of you to do. If, however, the situation persists, and you find that you are excluded time after time, then the harsh reality might be that your trio isn't working. It's no reflection on you—and it shouldn't stop you being friends with them individually—it's just the three-way friendship that isn't giving you what you want.

It's not all bad

Everyone will experience what it feels like to be the spare wheel at some point. It's pretty much a rite of passage into adulthood. People are complicated, and so are the relationships they form. Sometimes you will be the one everyone wants to know, and sometimes you won't. Being part of a trio can be challenging, but the reward of having two best friends to turn to instead of one can outweigh the difficulties. As the artist Andy Warhol once said, "One's company, two's a crowd, and three's a party."

WHAT TO DO IF YOUR TRIO BECOMES TOXIC

1 Step back to gain perspective
Take a deep breath and assess the situation objectively. Are your friends really going out much more without you, or are there just as many occasions when you're doing something with one of them, or when all three of you are out together? If they are seeing more of each other, could it be because they share an interest, or go to an after-school club together that's bringing them into closer contact?

2 Remember that relationships ebb and flow
The chances are your friendship triangle will shift and rebalance in a few weeks' time, so try to not let your concerns run away with you. Be patient and calm and give the situation time to resolve itself.

3 Try to let your friends know that you are feeling left out
Start by approaching the one you are closest to and talk to her face-to-face or on the phone rather than online. There's a good chance that they're not aware that they've hurt you, or that they don't realize how important it is to you to be included.

4 Think about how to modify your reaction
Being left out from time to time is inevitable—it happens to everyone. The important thing is not to take it too much to heart. And be careful not to make things worse by being standoffish, or by waiting for others to plan events that you can go along to. Take the initiative. See what's on at the movies and invite your friends.

5 Don't sit at home stalking them on social media
If they're out having a good time, then so should you be. Expand your friendship circle so that you have other people to socialize with. Having two best friends is great, but you shouldn't pin your whole social life on them and them alone.

SPEAK OUT

Public speaking can be a difficult skill to master, but with practice, it's possible to inspire a crowd with your spoken words

Are you afraid to state your opinion in class discussions? Or find yourself mumbling and stumbling over your words, losing your train of thought when asked to speak in front of others? You're not alone.

Many people have a fear of public speaking, experiencing some level of speech anxiety. Symptoms differ, from the common rapid heartbeat and butterflies in your stomach to incapacitating fear, an inability to get the words out, and uncontrollable hand shaking. Some people may look relaxed and confident, but this only comes with experience.

Underneath the surface, few are totally at ease. Like you, teachers, politicians, and celebrities feel anxious before a speech, but then a magical chain reaction takes place: As their speech progresses, their anxiety decreases and their confidence increases. The tricks? They learn to manage their nerves and, importantly, believe in their abilities. Knowing this, you, too, can shine with confidence...

HOW TO DELIVER CONFIDENT PRESENTATIONS

Be prepared
Firstly, choose a topic you're passionate about, making sure it fits the framework of the assignment. Start researching at least a few days before the big day and outline important information, as well as specific facts and opinions that may be difficult to memorize. Practice in front of a mirror or with a friend and use a stopwatch if you've been given a time limit.

Relax
Be aware of how you portray yourself and notice how you feel. Giving a speech can be nerve-racking so you need to acknowledge those feelings, understand they are normal, and employ a few helpful techniques (see the next page for some top tips). These methods have been proven to manage nerves so you can focus on communicating effectively.

Feel the excitement, not the fear
Don't ignore your fear. Instead, embrace it and transform the negative nervous energy into a positive one: Fear and excitement are closely intertwined as they involve the same chemicals in the body. If you think about it, the symptoms are the same (from the physical sensation in the stomach to the difficulty in sleeping), and it's actually your choice to interpret them either as fear or excitement.

Perfect your style…
Once you're in the right state of mind, you can look like a pro by holding your head high, smiling, and making eye contact with your audience (you may wish to find friendly faces in the crowd first). Speak loudly, slowly, and clearly, and don't be afraid to pause to stress a point. Engage with your audience, too, using amusing and extraordinary facts or simply by explaining why you're interested in the topic.

…but accept imperfection
Delivering a flawless speech is difficult, so don't worry if you make mistakes along the way. Most likely your audience won't notice them anyway, so don't focus on the imperfections and keep going gracefully. A nervous giggle or a mispronounced word is not the end of the world. Just take a deep breath and continue. Don't try to finish quickly and run away from what you may see as an embarrassing situation.

TOP TIPS

* Remember that speaking confidently in front of others takes practice, self-control, and self-belief. Most people aren't born with natural eloquence so confidence doesn't happen just like that—it's a mindset and takes effort to grow and maintain.

* Start by trying to define the cause of your anxiety. Are you afraid of forgetting what you need to say? Write a list of points you wish to discuss and practice your speech.

* Are you afraid that people will ask questions you won't be able to answer? Research your subject thoroughly, and if you don't know the answer, say so.

WAYS TO WOW YOUR AUDIENCE

Four simple ways to improve your speaking and presentation skills:

1 Share one thing no one knows
If you want people to engage and really listen to what you're saying, include something in your talk they didn't already know. An amazing fact, an unusual story, any piece of information you think they'll take away with them and tell others about.

2 Take a deep breath
Deep breaths are the secret to keeping calm. If you start to feel panicky, breathe deeply through your nose, hold your breath for a few seconds, then breathe out slowly from your mouth. Repeat until you feel relaxed.

3 Ask a question you can't answer
Ask a question you know the audience can't answer and then say: "That's okay. I can't either." Explain why you can't and then talk about what you do know. The audience will pay more attention and you'll come across as human and likeable for admitting you don't have all the answers.

4 Visualize your success
Envisioning your success beforehand can help. Before your next presentation, try closing your eyes and mentally taking yourself through everything—what you'll say, how the audience will react, and how pleased and proud you'll feel having delivered a great speech.

FRIEND OR FRENEMY?

What do you think of when you hear the word bully? An aggressive
person who physically hurts others? An older child who picks on
younger ones? When a bully is your worst enemy, it can be easy to
distance yourself from them. But what about when a bully is a friend?

Friends can sometimes be mean. They might be anxious about schoolwork, have issues at home, or be fretting about money. But what if their meanness is a regular thing and you're worried that if you stick up for yourself the friendship will start to break down? You might find yourself pretending everything's okay, even though deep down you know it's not. If the situation has been like this for a while, you may even feel stuck, that you can't change anything and it's scary even to try. But when a friend is more like an enemy—or a frenemy—it can eat away at your happiness and sense of well-being. Here's how you can take an honest look at friendships and tell when they're doing you more harm than good…

HOW TO SPOT A FRENEMY

It can be hard to admit that someone you consider to be a friend might be a frenemy. Sophie Elkan, author of *The Girls' Guide To Growing Up Great*, explains: "The confusing thing is that sometimes we can really like someone, even though we know deep down they aren't a good friend." In her book, Sophie describes behavior that might suggest you're in frenemy territory:

* If you feel you have to please them or do what they want to do

* If they try to persuade you to do things you're not comfortable with, such as breaking rules or being mean to others

* If they criticize your appearance

* If they're mean about your other friends or your family

* Frenemies might also be inconsistent, for example, being chatty and friendly one day and completely ignoring you the next

Katerina Georgiou, a counselor who is familiar with frenemy issues, recommends paying attention to how you feel after spending time with a friend. Do you feel refreshed or drained? Relaxed or stressed? Often you can't put your finger on it but you will come away from an encounter wondering why you're feeling a bit fragile, vulnerable, or defensive. She also advises thinking about how you feel with other friends, or groups of friends. Katerina says that although no friendship is perfect, if you feel consistently unhappy with one particular friend, then your friend might not be as friendly as they seem—they could be a frenemy.

UNDERSTANDING FRENEMIES

Frenemies can seem cool and charming on the surface, saying nice things about you that make you feel good about yourself—especially if they sing your praises in front of others. But as time goes on they become meaner.

Deep down, frenemies are often insecure. Criticizing others can be a tool that they use to make themselves feel good.

The thing is, if someone judges you and continually says mean things, it can hurt your self-esteem. You might even start believing what your friend says, which can draw you into a vicious cycle where you stick with them, hoping they'll come around and say nice things about you again.

It's important to remember that whatever a frenemy says and does reveals everything about them and nothing about who you really are.

"Better an honest enemy than a false friend"

Anon

WHAT TO DO ABOUT A FRENEMY

1 Talk it through
Firstly, confide in a trusted adult. Katerina suggests asking yourself how you'd feel if you were to talk through the issue with your frenemy. If you feel afraid, this is a red flag as you should be comfortable talking with friends. Be aware that a frenemy might deny anything's wrong. They might even blame you for the situation. This is why talking to an adult is important because it helps to gain an impartial perspective.

2 Set boundaries
It's important to say no to anything that makes you feel uncomfortable, even if this annoys your friend. If they don't change after you try to talk things through and set boundaries, then, as scary as it might be, it could be time to end the relationship.

3 Take a break
Don't ask other friends to take sides, but try to distance yourself from the frenemy. If they become mean or confrontational or go out of their way to make your life difficult, go back to your trusted adult and ask for support—you don't have to do this alone.

4 Make new friends
The best thing with facing the fear of losing your frenemy is that it allows for new friends to come along. Author Sophie says: "…truly, it is better to be on your own than to be with people who don't see how great you are and make you feel bad about yourself."

5 But remember…
Don't be too quick to point the finger. If someone's behavior has changed, it's also possible that something is going on in their life that you don't know about. It's always worth taking some time to evaluate your friendship before you make any big decisions.

GOODBYE TO GOSSIP

Gossiping behind someone's back is part of school life but can have devastating effects. Here's how you can address any malicious rumors that affect you...

"It's so obvious Ellie likes Sam! His girlfriend won't be happy when we tell her." ... "Did you see that photo of Sophie? She looks so fat in that top." ...

Gossip, or talking about other people and usually including facts that aren't true, is a huge part of school life. It could be one person passing on personal information about someone else to another friend—or at its worst, it could be a malicious rumor spread on social media sites. People who gossip often don't mean to hurt anyone—it's just their way of bonding and venting—but when gossip becomes personal and hurtful, it can be emotionally damaging and ruin self-esteem.

HOW TO DEAL WITH IT

It's very easy for people to tell you not to worry or ignore what others are saying, but it's hard not to care or be affected. It's true—and perhaps you can ignore it. Most gossip is forgotten quite quickly and, sadly, the gossips move on to a new victim. Being betrayed by friends, left out, lied about, or humiliated, however, can make you feel emotional, depressed, anxious, and angry. Here are a few ideas to help you move forward if you become the target of gossips…

1 Tell a friend
Talk to trusted friends about what's going on. You will feel better telling someone else and they can help you decide what is the best option to resolve the situation.

2 Write it down
Make a note of what's happened. Not only can writing down your thoughts and expressing how you're feeling help, but it is also good to document it in a journal. It could be you notice a pattern emerging, perhaps it's the same people or it occurs at certain times. If you can, get evidence—screenshot anything on social media.

3 Confront it
If you are brave enough, you could go to see the culprit who started the rumors and calmly ask if they did it and if so, why. You could explain the impact it has had on you. Think beforehand about what you want to say so you can clearly state your point without making things worse for yourself.

4 Know your truth
Be strong and stay positive about yourself. You know the truth and what kind of person you are. The gossips are the ones with the problem.

5 Avoid gossips
Stay away from people who gossip. If you find your friends are gossiping about others, either suggest that they stop, try to change the subject, or be friends with people who have better things to talk about.

6 Report it
If you feel the situation is affecting your mood or work, talk to a parent, teacher, or support worker. Being gossiped about can make you feel uncomfortable about going to school so your teachers will want to ensure this doesn't happen to you.

DEALING WITH
CYBERBULLIES

What can you do if you're threatened online?

Picture the scene: You happily post a new photo of yourself on Instagram™ only to find a few hours later that someone has made mean and hurtful comments and shared it. They've edited it with weird filters, added cruel words or emojis, or turned it into a meme, and reposted it. Hundreds of their followers that you don't know have laughed and liked it.

Imagine the hurt, the embarrassment, and the humiliation. Sadly, that feeling is experienced regularly (by people of all ages) and is just one kind of cyberbullying that leaves many feeling depressed, scared, and isolated.

Bullying has been around forever but cyberbullying is new. Before everyone had phones and the internet, teenagers who were bullied at school could leave their tormentors behind at the end of the day.

Cyberbullying can follow you home and continue even when you're alone in your bedroom. Shockingly, a children's charity recently announced it had recorded an 88 percent increase in calls about cyberbullying in the past five years—and usually these were a continuation of either physical or face-to-face emotional bullying.

One 13-year-old girl told a children's helpline: "Every day I wake up scared to go to school, scared about the comments people will make and scared about walking home. Then I get in and log onto my social networking site and there are horrible messages everywhere. It's like there's no escaping the bullies. I'm struggling to cope with how upset I feel so sometimes I cut myself just to have a release but it's not enough. I can't go on like this."

So what can you do if you are a victim of cyberbullying? And what should you do if you suspect someone is being a bully? Read on to find out.

WHAT COUNTS AS CYBERBULLYING?

Cyberbullying is any kind of bullying that takes place online or through phones or tablets. Places such as Facebook™, YouTube™, Instagram™, and Snapchat™ are supposed to be safe, fun places to be but sadly some people choose to go on there to threaten, harass, embarrass, or upset another person. Sometimes it's anonymous or done using fake profiles, which makes it even scarier. Often, the cyberbully will excuse their behavior as "banter"—but it is never a joke if the other person is upset. Other examples of cyberbullying include:

* Sending or posting threatening, abusive messages and comments.

* Stealing passwords and posing as the victim. Sometimes, bullies trick people into revealing information and then post it on other sites or share it.

* Creating websites, profiles, or blogs either posing as the target or making hateful or cruel untrue comments about them.

What can you do if you are being cyberbullied?

1 Tell someone. Like face-to-face bullying, cyberbullying can make you feel low, anxious, and helpless. Too often, people are scared to open up about what's going on for fear it will make it worse, but it is important to let someone know. No one has the right to bully you—you have the right to feel safe online and people can help you stop the bullying. Tell a parent or a trusted adult, perhaps a teacher or school support worker.

2 Save or take a screenshot of all the messages if you can so the adults helping you can ensure the bully is dealt with properly. It may be that the police get involved and they will need evidence.

3 Report harassing comments and fake profiles on whatever social media platform you use. There are always ways to report content.

How can you stop it happening to you?

You have a right to feel safe on social media, while using your phones and visiting websites but sadly, there will always be bullies out there. You can, however, protect yourself in some ways.

One key piece of advice is—think before you post! You probably hear this a lot but it's true. Don't share passwords, photos, or information you wouldn't want your grandma or teachers to see or know online, not even with friends. This doesn't mean you can't post photos, just always be careful who you share with and consider who is on your friends list too. Is there anyone who might be inclined to repost or share your information or picture in a way that might be hurtful?

Also, look into the privacy controls on the websites or messaging programs you use—you can control who sees your profile and who can contact you.

What can you do if you think you know cyberbullying is going on?

* **Report it** You can pass on any harassment you see to the social media site but you can also tell a trusted adult about what is going on.

* **Help the person being bullied** Send them a private message and tell them you don't agree with what is happening. If you are brave and it is safe to do so, post a positive comment publicly to the target.

How can you ensure you aren't accused of being a cyberbully?

When you make comments about someone else, imagine how you'd feel if someone said that about you. Often people make offensive comments online without meaning to be hurtful, but "banter" can be misinterpreted or easily turned into something more serious. Don't participate, like, or share posts that bully another person.

If you think you are or have been a cyberbully… stop. Your actions are hurting someone. If you post abuse about anyone online or if you send threats, you can be traced by the police and could be guilty of a criminal offence.

Often, there is a reason in someone's past that pushes them toward becoming a bully. If you think this is you, you can change. Tell an adult and ask for their help.

BOLD AND BEAUTIFUL

Sometimes putting other people's needs before your own is necessary, but if you're constantly making life easier for those around you at the expense of your own opinions and desires, it could be time for a change

One of your friends makes a comment you don't agree with, a store overcharges you, or a teacher misunderstands you, what would your response be? Perhaps you'd get annoyed but shy away from saying anything, or maybe you'd be at the other end of the spectrum altogether, ranting and raving at anyone who will pay you attention.

Being assertive means getting the balance right between being too quiet and passive, or too loud and aggressive. Assertive behavior acknowledges your needs—as well as those of others—and communicates what they are without apologizing, either for them or your emotions.

Your may feel your assertiveness skills aren't too strong at the moment, but the good news is they can be developed and refined, so you can stand your ground and show the people around you that your thoughts and feelings matter too.

Notice your patterns

The first step in developing assertiveness is to start looking at patterns of behaviors and responses. Recognizing that you go along with what other people want or think is often a key feature in passivity and means your needs are rarely met. Over time, this approach can build resentment, which can come out in angry bursts.

At the other end, do you notice yourself flying off the handle when you don't get your way or someone doesn't agree with everything you're saying? Everyone does it, but it seldom leaves you feeling good and, importantly, the other person probably stopped listening as soon as you got angry. Keep a note of your responses so you can see if there's a pattern emerging.

Watch your communication

In her book, *Presence*, Amy Cuddy suggests that powerful speech is a vital part of assertiveness and confidence. Rather than speaking quietly and rushing through what you're trying to say, this involves speaking up so others can hear you properly, making eye contact, and taking your time. It's okay to pause and speak slowly.

Once you've spent some time practicing this behavior, look again at the words you're using. Are you forever apologizing or keeping your true feelings to yourself? Tune in to how you're really feeling in your thoughts and emotions and watch out for physical signals from your body that can alert you to changing emotions (think butterflies in your stomach or your chest tightening).

Take a deep breath and share how you feel in response to someone else's behavior. Then (here's the really brave bit) tell them how you'd like things to be different. Try using the "I feel… when you… I would like…" framework in your conversation. For example, you might say: "I feel sad when you don't invite me to your sleepovers. I'd really like us to hang out more again."

What's your body language saying?

Even if your words sound more assertive, what's your body language telling the outside world? Other people will be able to work out your feelings from the way you hold your body and the manner in which you move.

Passive body language often involves sloping forward, and hanging your shoulders and head. You might walk slowly, have your arms crossed, and make small movements.

Assertive body language displays confidence without aggression. According to Amy, this means standing up tall and straight; making big open gestures, such as having your arms out wide; standing rather than sitting when appropriate; and even placing your hands on your hips.

Our panel (below) has some poses you can practice before going into a new environment, before a difficult conversation, or just when you need a boost.

Start believing you matter

While these tips can help to make huge strides toward assertiveness, the final ingredient is to start believing that you truly matter and that what you think and say really is important.

Developing your assertiveness is a way of taking some responsibility for your own needs and it signals to others how to treat you. The time for sinking into the shadows has passed, it's time to stand up and be counted and let the world know that you've arrived.

POWER POSES

Wonder woman Place your hands on hips, keep your feet hip-distance apart, your chin slightly lifted.
Outstretched arms Imagine you've just won a race, put your arms up in a wide "V" in the air as if celebrating.
Superman Place your feet hip-distance apart, one hand on your hip, your other arm straight up in the air with fist clenched.

Hold the pose for at least 30 seconds. Try them when no one's watching— they might seem silly at first, but they can help you feel more powerful.

THE AGE OF ANXIETY

Do you often feel anxious or stressed? If not, perhaps you have a friend or relative who feels this way. Social media, excessive use of the internet, gaming, peer pressure, family issues, and exams are some of the reasons given for feeling under pressure, anxious, or unable to relax.

If you do ever feel anxious, you don't have to suffer in silence and think there's nothing that can help. Try some of these suggestions to help regain some inner peace and feel ready to take on the world again…

1 Be kind
It's important to stop being hard on yourself. Imagine the advice you'd give to a friend who confided they felt the way you do at the moment, and then take your own advice. If you'd suggest they speak to someone else who might be able to help, pamper themselves, or just stop worrying so much about what others think —do this yourself.

2 Plan treats
Ensure you have nice days or evenings planned for future days and weeks so you have events to look forward to. It could be catching up with an old friend, heading to the movies to watch an exciting release, getting a new hairstyle, or cooking something you really love. Having something positive on the calendar will raise your spirits.

3 Turn off your phone
For a few hours, have no access to the internet or social media. At first, it will feel difficult, but the more you do it, the more you'll realize how stressed all those constant refreshes and updates can make you and how much time you spend looking at the screen. You'll also realize you don't need it as much as you think. It's also a good idea not to have your phone near you at night as this can interrupt your sleep. Give your brain a break and occupy it with other things, such as reading, meditation, yoga, exercise, or sleep.

> *"In every life we have some trouble,*
> *but when you worry you make it double"*

Bobby McFerrin

4 Get outside

It's easy to forget how much of a lift you can get from being outside in fresh air and nature, so try to give yourself some time to take notice of it. Go for a walk somewhere nice, take your dog out, or go to the park and read, taking in the nature and fresh air around you. Make a point of really noticing all the things around you that you might not always appreciate.

5 Breathe

Focusing on your breathing will help you slow down your mind and reduce feelings of tension and anxiety. With the tip of your tongue resting just behind your teeth, inhale through the nose for the count of four, hold for six, and exhale slowly through the mouth. Repeating this several times will relax you and also help your mind and body.

6 Let go of worries

Time is often wasted worrying about things you've said or done. Remember, you can't do anything about the past apart from learn from it. That one spelling mistake in your homework—it doesn't matter now. Instead, consider all the good things you've done. Another thing you might worry about is what others, often people you barely know, think. If this is you, focus only on your opinions and those of your closest family and friends. You can't change other people's minds about you or what you do, look like, or wear, but you can change how you deal with it.

7 Sleep

Ensure you get the sleep you need. Have a regular bedtime and wake-up time and try not to look at your phone before going to sleep. Also avoid hot showers or baths just before sleep as you need a while to cool down before getting your Zs. If your phone is still nearby, you could use it to try a podcast or app that has soothing sounds or listen to some guided help to help you relax.

8 Food for thought

Some foods and drinks can raise anxiety levels. If you're stressed, try not to have too many caffeine-packed coffees and hot chocolates or sugar-rich sweets. Instead, opt for food deemed as calming or anxiety reducing, such as yogurt, bananas, and dark leafy greens.

9 Write it down

Make a list of the things that are stressing you at the moment and then start to consider how you can tackle each one in turn. Perhaps share the list with someone you trust so they can help you explore what you could do. Writing things down is also a great way to release anxiety and give you some clarity of thought. You might want to set yourself a few minutes a day to note stressful thoughts and only allow yourself to worry during this time.

10 Know when to get help

If your anxiety doesn't improve and starts affecting your everyday life, speak to your parents, teachers, or doctor who will be able to advise you where to get help. There are many organizations out there who have experience of helping people who get anxious and will be able to assist you. Remember: You aren't alone, so never suffer in silence.

BEATING BETRAYAL

How to cope when those you trust break your confidence

Being betrayed is one of the most painful feelings in the world. When it happens to you, it can shake you to your core, affect your ability to trust others, and leave you feeling vulnerable and exposed.

Betrayal can come in many forms, but ultimately it's when someone you love and trust does something that hurts you deeply. You may feel betrayed if your parents split up or start seeing other people; a friend reveals your secrets; or someone talks about you behind your back. It can leave you angry and questioning your relationship with the person who's hurt you. It can also damage your faith in others as you end up wondering if they'll betray you next.

Why do people hurt those they love?

There isn't a definitive answer to why people betray others. People change, people make mistakes. Sometimes those you love aren't the people you think they are. Betrayal means the deliberate act of hurting someone (and when someone betrays you it reflects on them, not on your worth), but sometimes you may feel betrayed even when the person who has upset you hasn't done it with that intention.

People who betray others are often overcome by a sense of ambition, greed, or passion and when they can't control these things, they may do something that causes them to betray those they love. For example, a friend's desire to be part of the in-crowd could mean they reveal secrets or share information given to them in strictest confidence just so they can get into the group.

When someone is determined to do or get something, nothing can stand in their way—even if it means betraying those closest to them. In relationships, powerful emotions can change people and make them behave differently.

WAYS TO OVERCOME THE PAIN OF BETRAYAL

1 Don't bottle up your feelings
If you don't discuss how the betrayal has made you feel, it might have negative effects in the future. For example, it could disrupt your sleep patterns, affect your mental health, or prevent you trusting others. Feeling betrayed hurts, so allow yourself to cry, shout, and think about the situation for a while. It's natural to be upset in these circumstances.

2 Write it down
Take the time you need to consider what emotions you're experiencing and write down how you feel. You may also want to write a letter to the person who's hurt you, explaining exactly how you feel—but don't send it. Wait a week or so and re-read it before deciding whether or not to pass it on as you may find your feelings have changed, too. Even if the letter is solely for your own eyes, you'll find that just writing the words down can make you feel better.

3 Avoid retaliating
It's normal to want to get revenge on the person who betrayed you, but don't react quickly. Actions and words that come from a place of anger and hurt could be ones you end up regretting. Take time to process what's gone on and think the situation through. Look after yourself first.

4 Talk to someone
Discussing the situation can help you clear your mind and start the healing process. If you're finding it hard to get over the hurt and feel it's affecting you and that you can't switch off from it, talk to a trusted adult—it might be a guardian, an aunt or uncle, or the school counselor—who will be able to advise you.

5 Forgive and forget?
This may seem hard but, depending on the circumstances and how much the person means to you, give it time—it will benefit your well-being if you're able to forgive the person involved. It doesn't mean you accept what they did is right or forget it—but it will allow you some control of the situation in your mind and help you to move on. If you have hate and anger in your head for too long, it can end up hurting you more than you realize. And remember, just because one person has betrayed you, it doesn't mean everyone will. Surround yourself with positive, honest friends to remind yourself that betrayal is rare.

HANDS UP—I WAS WRONG

Everyone gets something wrong or makes a mistake at some point in their life, so why is it so difficult to own up to an innocent blunder?

It can be an awful feeling when you realize you've said or done something wrong. Maybe you shared a piece of incorrect gossip about the new student in your class, told a friend something that turned out to be totally false, or gave someone the wrong date for a special event which meant they missed out. Whatever the reason for being wrong, having to admit it, often with an apology, can make your stomach churn, your face flush, and your pulse race.

No one relishes putting up their hand to say: "I was wrong." You become accountable for your mistake and that can make you feel awkward, embarrassed, ashamed, and less than perfect. Admitting a mistake challenges your pride and can dent your ego. Saying you were wrong means having to accept that you're not always right or perfect, and that can feel deeply uncomfortable.

Of course, having a sense of pride in yourself isn't a bad thing. When you take pride in your good qualities, abilities, appearance, and achievements, it's positive and encourages healthy feelings of self-worth. Problems arise when you have an inflated opinion of yourself and become too proud to admit, and take responsibility for, your mistakes.

> "Mistakes are always forgivable, if one has the courage to admit them"

Bruce Lee

Stubborn pride

When pride rules, you believe you're always right, even when you're proven wrong. Stubborn pride foolishly protects a built-in need to be seen as being perfect. It can make you self-righteous and your ego will simply not stand down or admit failure. To do so would reveal your flaws and weaknesses and your pride doesn't want this.

As a result, some people will go to great lengths to avoid owning up to being wrong. They will deny, make excuses, attack, or blame someone or something else because it's easier than looking within and finding they're at fault.

No one likes an arrogant "know-it-all," especially one who never confesses to being wrong. This unattractive side of being too proud to admit your mistakes has an impact on yourself and others. It can ruin friendships and spoil experiences. Relationships are at risk, leading to a loss of trust, love, and respect. It can fill you with angst and even guilt for not doing what you know is right—and this, in turn, can damage your self-worth in the long run.

Strength of character

Imagine switching off your pride for a moment and focus purely on the facts of a situation that has resulted in you making a mistake. When you look upon the matter objectively, without consequence to yourself, it's usually plain to see the right course of action to take. When you can say you were wrong and offer a genuine apology, it will help to clear up a situation that might otherwise linger on for years and tarnish your memories.

Owning up to your mistake and taking responsibility means that you can move forward with a clear conscience.

Finding the courage to say you were wrong will feel like a burden has been lifted. There is a certain dignity in showing that you can rise above your personal pride and do the right thing. It demonstrates integrity, authenticity, and strength of character. It shows that you value your relationships over the importance of being right.

This vulnerability and humility makes you more approachable. People will see you in a fresh light. It will earn you respect, trust, and admiration, and will enable you to grow into a well-rounded individual.

So, don't be afraid to make mistakes and don't be too proud to say you got it wrong. You are human and on a beautiful, but sometimes challenging, journey that will often test you. Keep your pride in check, have the courage to do what feels right, and learn from experience.

TIME TO REFLECT

Take a few moments to consider when pride has stopped you from saying and doing the right thing:

* When was the last time you felt too proud to own up to your mistake and say you were wrong?

* By not admitting you said or did something wrong, what happened (or didn't happen) as a result?

* How did this make you feel?

* What could you have said to change the situation?

STAND OUT FROM THE CROWD

Do you think for yourself? Parents, social media, teachers, friends, television—with so many outside influences, how do you know what to believe and who is right? Here's why questioning those around you can sometimes be a good thing

Some days it can feel like everyone is telling you what to think. It could be your parents, friends, ads on television, books, or social media—all telling you how to dress, what you should be buying, what to listen to, and who to follow.

Every now and then it's important to take a step back and reflect on where your influences come from. This doesn't mean taking the opposite view just to stand out, or that all your ideas have to be original. It just means that whatever beliefs or opinions you hold have been well thought out, by you. It's about learning to think critically about what you want to believe and who you want to be.

WHAT IS CRITICAL THOUGHT?

Thinking critically just means questioning everything. If someone tells you something as a fact, don't be afraid to ask them where they got their information from. Sure, if you quiz your teachers every time they tell you something they might get a bit annoyed (it doesn't mean you shouldn't do it), but if it is an opinion on a subject you should feel free to ask a few questions, especially if it's friends and family.

This isn't quite as easy when it comes to media like television or the internet. If you start asking the TV where it got its facts, the TV probably won't answer back! If you hear or read something that you're not sure about, search for it online, ask different people about it, and form your own opinion.

If you like a certain type of music that your friends may not like, don't let them tell you not to listen to it. It's the thing you like, how could it be bad? And if your friends like a certain type of music, it doesn't mean that you have to. Listen to it, but ask yourself whether you like it just because they do.

Why is it important?

Forming your own opinions not only helps you figure out what is true and what is false, but it will make you happier and a more interesting person in the long run. What would the art world be without Picasso? Or music be without The Beatles? All great artists are just people who decided to go their own way.

Learning to think independently will help you to develop your unique character. Spending less time on social media might help you to feel better about yourself without the need for acceptance online. You may find that you become a stronger, more self-reliant person. So remember, question everything, and if anyone asks why you're always asking questions, ask them why they don't like you asking questions!

HOW TO BE YOUR OWN PERSON

1 Going off grid

There's no need to delete all forms of social media. You might regret that when no one knows how to get in touch with you. Instead, try a weekend detox. Or make it a week, or a day, or even just limiting the time you spend online.

2 Gather information

Don't let other people's opinions change your own until you've thought about it for yourself. Whether it is one friend complaining about another or your favorite celebrity sharing their opinions on Twitter™, try to get as much information from different people as possible and use this to form your own opinion.

3 Be open to trying something new

Just because your friends enjoy something, it doesn't mean that you must. Trying a new hobby is a great way to make new friends, and can lead to fun and interesting adventures.

4 Be wary of influences in the media

Listicles giving you bite-size information, ads hidden in YouTube™ videos, products posted on Instagram™—the internet is full of information trying to influence your opinions. If you can't avoid the media online, try to look critically at what they're saying and why they're saying it. Keeping an eye out for advertising can really help you understand what you like and what you're being told to like.

5 Be confident in who you are

Don't be afraid to be yourself. People may try to tell you that you're doing something wrong, or that what you're doing is different or weird, but remember that one person's weirdness is fascinating for someone else. Interests that other people don't enjoy can lead to the most rewarding hobbies.

A LION'S ROAR

The lion has been a symbol of strength, courage, honor, nobility, and pride since ancient times, with a roar that can be heard up to five miles away. The lion pose, which is called Simhasana in Sanskrit, is a powerful breathing exercise that helps you express yourself and stand your ground

How to perform lion pose:

1 Sit in a kneeling position, back straight and upright, shoulders opening backward, palms resting on thighs, above the knee, fingers spread like lion claws.

2 Breathe in all the way up to the crown of your head, maintaining a straight spine, shoulders rounded back, chest wide.

3 Breathing out, gently lean your body forward, open your mouth wide, stick your tongue out long and flat pointing downward toward the ground, making a strong "*Ha*" sound. Simultaneously as your tongue flows out and downward, your gaze flows skyward up through the middle of your eyes.

4 On completion, bring your tongue back into your mouth, close it, bring your eyes back to looking forward, and straighten your spine into a seated upright position.

5 Repeat this breath for about five or 10 breaths and observe how you feel.

Experiment with this breath and your body. One variation is to practice breathing as above, but this time have your knees open wide with your palms on the floor (wrists turned so that your fingers are pointing back toward your body). Breathing in, tilt your upper body forward, pushing downward through your arms. Then, breathing out, stick your tongue out flat pointing downward.

"I breathe in my courage and exhale my fear"

Anon

JUST SAY NO

Resisting peer pressure can be tough, but it's not impossible. Stand your ground and be confident about who you are and what you want to do

Whether it's wearing your hair a certain way, being mean to another classmate, lying to someone, or drinking alcohol, at some point in your life, you will feel pushed toward making a certain choice by one or more of your friends. What kind of person are you? Do you say yes for a quiet life, give in and do what they say, or say no and stick to what you feel is right?

Most of your peers—another word for someone your own age—will have a hugely positive influence on your life without you realizing it, from being good role models to helping you out. But there'll be others who start pushing you to do things you might not want to. It can be hard to say no, especially when you want to fit in. Some students may say "yes" because they are afraid of losing friends or they don't want to hurt a person's feelings—or even because they aren't sure what they really want. Everyone gives in to pressure at some point, but unless you want to give in every time you face it, it's good to learn how to handle it.

DON'T WORRY WHAT OTHERS THINK

Get to know the true you What do you really like? What are your hopes, dreams, and ambitions? Are you doing things because you want to, or because they'll please or impress someone else?

Don't be a mind reader You can't know what others are thinking, and they're probably thinking a lot less about you than you might imagine.

Let go of perfect Doing and saying everything right is not the way to be liked or respected—it's those most confident to be themselves who are usually the most popular.

TOP TIPS FOR DEALING WITH TRICKY PEER PRESSURE SITUATIONS

1 Just say no

This is the obvious one, but it can be tough to do. If you aren't comfortable with what's being asked of you, say "no" and back it up with a positive statement such as, "I'm okay, thanks." If they keep on at you, say it assertively but not aggressively. It will be hard but if they're your real friends, they won't make demands of you.

2 Walk away

If you're finding saying no isn't working, walk away from the situation. Remember the reasons you don't want to be involved and stick to your beliefs. If your peers are going to do something, they can do it without you. Don't fall for the line "everyone's doing it." They're not.

3 Buddy up

If you're feeling uncomfortable, it's likely others are too and are probably hoping someone else will feel the same and be braver than them. It helps to have another friend who's also willing to say no and who'll back you up, so if someone says no, back them up. Otherwise be the brave one—your real friends will thank you for it. Using words that link you with others in the group can help: "We don't want to..." or, "Let's go do something else," or even, "Leave her alone, she said she didn't want any."

4 Stick up for yourself

If you can, let the person pressurizing you know how you feel. Stand up straight, make eye contact, and tell them why you don't want to do what they're asking. You don't have to make excuses for your own opinions. The most popular people are often the ones who aren't afraid to say how they feel or do what they want.

5 Unspoken pressure

Some people feel pressure just from being around others, seeing how they act or dress or wear their makeup, and feeling they should be the same. It could be that you look up to celebrities or family members who do things such as drink or smoke and feel you should be like them. Remember, you are an individual and have control over your choices. Be yourself!

6 Avoid stressful situations

Steer clear of being alone with people who you know could put pressure on you. Likewise with tricky situations. For example, if there's a party with alcohol or drugs and you know you may be pushed into taking part or doing something that you don't want to, make your excuses not to go.

7 Choose your friends wisely

You may have had people say to you "choose your friends wisely." It is important to pick friends who have the same morals and values as you—and most importantly friends who won't make you do things you don't want to. If they don't respect your wishes not to, it may be time to rethink your friendship group and find some who do. You deserve friends who will listen and look out for you.

8 Be your own best friend

Be confident about who you are and trust your values and choices. Focus on being the best version of you that you can be instead of wanting to fit in with others. If you're feeling pushed and are struggling to say no, find a friend, parent, or teacher and let them know how you feel. It's good to get advice from others.

9 Support positive peer pressure

Sometimes peer pressure can be used to do good, such as encouraging bullies to treat people better or to motivate others to get behind a cause you feel passionately about. Think of a time when a friend pushed you to do something good for yourself or to avoid something that would have been bad. How could you and your friends use good pressure to help each other?

GHOSTED

What should you do when a friend suddenly ignores you?

It's a common experience: Last week, you and your friend were hanging out after school, making plans for the weekend, and endlessly texting. Suddenly, your friend is barely acknowledging your existence—your messages go unanswered and they're avoiding you at school.

Why is this happening?

This behavior is easier to understand, even if not easy to deal with, when there's a clear reason for it—if you've had an argument, for example. What's harder to handle is when your friend's sudden cold treatment has come from nowhere. You scroll back through message threads and rummage in the corners of your mind for signs of recent trouble—only to draw a blank. What's going on?

It's important to realize that a friendship, like any relationship, has its ups and downs. Sometimes, a friend ghosting you may just be one of those downs. As hurtful as this feels, it may be a phase in the friendship's natural pattern. That said, your feelings matter, so it's important to identify what's going on and how you can either improve the situation or, if that's not possible, protect yourself against it.

How do I know if I'm being ghosted?

Being ghosted can take many forms. Are you being ignored? Is your friend consistently failing to answer your messages or return your calls? Are they walking straight past you without uttering a word or turning their back on you in a group situation and talking very obviously about things or events in which you're not involved? Being totally shunned in this way, both publicly and privately, can be upsetting and humiliating.

Trickier to interpret are actions involving delay—like when you message a friend and they take a lot longer than usual to reply, or when you suggest doing something together and they respond vaguely, rather than enthusiastically.

There's no sense in getting anxious if this happens once or twice—after all, everybody has times when their phone is dead or they have to check other commitments before they can give a definite answer.

Similarly, if you find yourself face to face and your friend acts unnaturally or appears to make excuses to end the encounter, don't fret—they may just have other things on their mind. If a pattern starts to emerge, however, it may be that your friend is taking a deliberate step back from your friendship. Either way, be sure to weigh it all up carefully before jumping to conclusions.

What's going on with them?

As hurt or abandoned as you feel, take a moment to put yourself in the other person's shoes. Could they be going through a really busy or stressful time? Are they shutting down because something is causing them distress? Even if you haven't had a fight, have you said or done something that's made its way back to them? Try to think about your actions objectively: Something that you consider harmless could have been interpreted differently by your friend.

What should I do?

Accusing your friend of ghosting you could potentially make the situation worse. So, tempting as it may be to bombard them with messages and questions, it may be better to give them space. Instead of an approach that may come across as defensive or aggressive ("Why are you ignoring me?"), try something more along the lines of "You don't seem yourself. Is everything okay?" This gives your friend the opportunity to explain the situation to you. If they don't want to elaborate, it may be worth stepping back for a little while.

Safeguard yourself in all of this, too. It's considerate to give your friend time and space, but what about you? That time and space should not, at your end, be filled with fretting about what's going on.

Making time for yourself and what you enjoy is always important, but never more so than when you need to shield yourself from things you have no control over. Seek out other friends, engage in other hobbies, indulge in other treats. Get on with your life.

Rumination, obsession, and stalking on social media are absolutely not your friends right now. Don't write off your friendship with that person, but don't let this situation consume you or define this moment in your life.

What can you learn from this?

There are life lessons to be learned from the bumps in the road of every relationship. For one thing, you learn you cannot control the behaviors of others.

These situations also give you an opportunity to examine your own behaviors, and you do have control over these. Do you sometimes push people away because you fear they're going to abandon you first? Are your friendships properly balanced or are you often in a position where you feel you hold less "power"? This time of separation from the other person is a good space in which to look for patterns and think about ways to alter them.

"Fake friends believe in rumors,
real friends believe in you"

Anon

When you talk again

In most cases, being ghosted is temporary. If you still value your friendship and want it to continue, try to make the first few interactions you have afterward face-to-face ones—texts are easily misinterpreted.

Be honest about how the episode has made you feel. If you know that you've done nothing wrong, don't apologize just to get things back to normal, as you'll be helping to create a dynamic of imbalance in the future—and most likely setting yourself up for repeat episodes of blame.

If, however, you can see that you're at fault in some way, accept and acknowledge that responsibility and apologize for it sincerely. This is a time to reboot your friendship, to make it work for both of you, and to look to the future.

TALK TO ME!

How do you start a conversation with people you don't know?

Meeting new people can be a nerve-racking experience, especially if you're shy. You might think you have to come across as the life and soul of the party or feel under pressure to be interesting and funny, but the truth is that most people feel daunted around new people. Some are just better at acting confidently—and this can be you, too. Even if you don't feel self-assured, you can learn to act as if you are until it comes naturally the more you get to know someone.

How you start conversations will depend on the situation. If it's somewhere with a group of people, take some time listening and start by asking questions based on what they're discussing. If it's just you and someone else, one of you will have to be brave and instigate a chat. A few handy conversation starters will help. You don't need to have a script, but just a few lines to ensure you aren't feeling out of your depth in those potentially awkward situations…

WHAT SHOULD I SAY?

Speaking with strangers needn't be scary. Here are some ideas to get you started:

Try giving someone a compliment and following it up with a question

* I love your top. Do you mind me asking where you got it from?
* Your hair is amazing. Where do you get it done?
* I enjoyed your speech in class the other day. Were you nervous?
* You seem always to do well in French class. What's your secret?

Break the ice

* How is your day going?
* What do you think of the party so far?
* How do you know him/her?
* This weather is awful, isn't it?
* Have you traveled far to be here?

Find some things you have in common

* Is this your first time here?

* What are your favorite sports?

* Where do you go to school?

* What would be your dream vacation?

* What kind of music do you listen to?

* What do you want to do when you leave school?

"Would you rather…" questions are always a sure-fire way to get to know people

* Would you rather win the lottery or have superpowers?

* Would you rather live in a country that was too hot or too cold?

* Would you rather give up the internet or your friends for a year?

* Would you rather fly or read minds?

* Would you rather eat only chocolate for the rest of your life or never eat it again?

TOP TALKING TIPS

1 Introduce yourself, if necessary
Consider how you come across. If you don't know the person, introduce yourself with a smile and friendly face, relax your posture, consider your body language, make eye contact, and show you are listening and are interested. People love to feel others are enjoying their stories.

2 Be confident
You can get tongue-tied if you feel you're nervous or too boring or unimportant to speak to someone. Try to relax and remind yourself that the person you're talking to might be feeling nervous, too—and even if you do stumble over words, no one will remember. Most people won't rush to judge you and instead will be happy to chat.

3 Listen up!
It's important to remember that being interesting doesn't always mean you have to leave the biggest impression or tell the best stories—it means you leave a good impression on people, engaging with the conversation and being a good listener, too. Don't worry if you're not a great conversationalist—ask some questions and try to be a sounding board.

4 Brush up your knowledge
If you already know the people you're meeting but haven't seen them for a long time, look on social media to see what they've been up to and use anything they've posted as a conversation starter. They'll be glad you've shown an interest.

5 Newsflash
Even with people you don't know, you should be able to discuss something that's happened in the news lately as a conversation starter. You could try: "What's your opinion on…?" or "Did you hear about…?" The weather is always a useful topic to fall back on if all else fails!

6 Be sensitive to others
You should get a good idea quite quickly if the other person is interested in your chat. It may be they don't want to talk or don't feel comfortable with the questions you're asking. Try to be thoughtful and change the subject or, failing that, accept they aren't particularly chatty—or perhaps friendly—people.

STEP INTO THE

SPOTLIGHT

From singing to plate-spinning, performing live on stage is a test of nerves as well as talent, but overcoming fears can boost your confidence

Does the thought of performing live on stage fill your stomach with gently apprehensive fluttering butterflies or let's-get-out-of-here flapping bats? Neither? That might be because for many it's a combination of both as worries about personal ability mix with excitement at the thought of putting on a great show.

But it's time to try to put all this to one side because evidence shows that participation in the arts can help to boost self-esteem and help you to become the person you aspire to be.

There are many reasons people fear stepping up as a performer including worry about lack of talent, shyness, concerns about forgetting lines or dance moves, and even doubts that the performing arts are a worthwhile pursuit.

But every performer of stage and screen started from a similar point and many successful artists including singers Adele, Beyoncé, and Rhianna, and actors Keira Knightley and Megan Fox, have experienced stage fright in their careers. Any fresh challenge is likely to bring out uncertainties and self-doubts. What's important is to acknowledge these feelings and then go ahead and take that first step regardless.

Class act

It helps to have encouraging and supportive people around you, be that parents, teachers, or friends. If your school doesn't have a drama program think about signing up for singing, drama, or dance classes. There are many amateur dramatic groups and choirs who welcome beginners or young people learning the trade.

REASONS TO PERFORM

* Enhances self-esteem and self-confidence
* Improves your communication and presentation skills
* Encourages imaginative thinking and creativity
* Helps you to face challenging situations
* Overcomes shyness, self-doubt, and fear
* Helps you to become more resilient and self-disciplined
* Improves coordination and resourcefulness
* Promotes greater self-belief and enjoyment of life
* Gives satisfaction from improving your performance and sharing your talent

ALL YOU NEED TO KNOW ABOUT STAGE FRIGHT

If you find yourself almost paralyzed by nerves before or during a performance, there are things you can do…

* Breathe. Slowly inhale and exhale. Feel calmness at the core of your being

* Jump up and down for a few moments to shake out any anxiety

* Relax, eat healthy food, and get enough sleep before a performance

* See your audience as wonderful friends who want you to succeed

* Rather than thinking of what might go wrong, focus on the positive and believe you have what it takes to give your best

* Replace any fear by focusing on the fun of performing and the enjoyment you're providing to spectators

* Practice makes you better prepared. And the more prepared you are, the better you will perform

* Always be yourself. Performing allows you to take on many different characters, but don't forget to let your personality shine through

Find out more
There are dozens of performing arts groups and societies to be found online. For more information, check out organizations like Americans for the Arts (americansforthearts.org) and GuideStar (guidestar.org).

READING ALOUD

When you think about reading aloud, do you feel shy at
the thought of speaking in front of classmates, or warm
and happy as you remember being read to before bed? Maybe a
little of both. But did you know this simple practice can also give you
confidence, make you laugh, and even improve your memory?

Try reading this aloud…
If you ever go to tea with my Aunty Mabel,
Never put your elbows on the dining-room table,
Always wipe your shoes if you've been in the garden,
Don't ever burp. If you do, say pardon.

Jeanne Willis, *Poems To Perform*

ARE YOU SMILING YET? HERE ARE SOME MORE REASONS TO READ ALOUD…

1 Reading aloud makes you notice the words on the page far more than when you
read them in your head. You think about when to pause (to make people listen
more closely), when to speed up (to add excitement), when to speak more loudly
(to emphasize what you're saying).

2 You become a better listener, so you are able to really hear yourself, which can
lead to you discovering your own unique writing voice.

3 Reading aloud is great practice for public speaking, helping you to enunciate
your words and feel less self-conscious in front of others.

4 When you read your own work out loud it allows you to pick up mistakes you
may not have noticed—a missing comma, a boring passage, a wrong word.

5 The more you do it, the better your visual memory becomes—the ability to see
images in your mind.

SO, ARE YOU SITTING COMFORTABLY?
THEN LET'S BEGIN...

* Start with a few sentences from a book or poem that you like. You will be surprised how quickly your voice gains in strength and confidence once you start reading. You may need several attempts before it becomes fluent and natural, so don't worry if you stumble at first.

* Think about the shape of your mouth and the way it moves to say words clearly. Try recording yourself. Does it sound like you thought it would? Do you speak clearly? Or do your words run into one another?

* Choose what to read to suit your mood. If you need a boost, pick words that inspire warmth and happiness. If you need cheering up, find a writer who you know can make you smile.

WHEN TO SAY THE WORDS

1 To feel more brave
Reading aloud can be a powerful tool if you are seeking inspiration or courage.

"If ever there is tomorrow when we're not together… there is something you must always remember. You're braver than you believe, stronger than you seem, and smarter than you think."
Winnie-the-Pooh

Margery Williams' *The Velveteen Rabbit* hides an inspirational message about learning to be yourself within its pages. It becomes even more powerful when read aloud. Give it a try. What do you think?

"It doesn't happen all at once," he said. "You become. It takes a long time. That's why it doesn't often happen to people who break easily, or have sharp edges, or who have to be carefully kept. Generally, by the time you are Real, most of your hair has been loved off, and your eyes drop out and you get loose in the joints and very shabby. But these things don't matter at all, because once you are Real you can't be ugly, except to people who don't understand."

2 For fun with friends
What about an evening of ghost stories? A sleepover can be the perfect time for reading hair-raising stories out loud, fun and not as frightening when your friends are near.

"The more that you read, the more things you will know. The more that you learn, the more places you'll go"

Dr. Seuss, *I Can Read With My Eyes Shut*

3 To practice for school

How do you feel relaxed when it's your turn to get up and speak? Nothing works as well as as a tongue-twister for loosening the lips or a nonsense rhyme to make you smile. Julia Donaldson's fabulous *Poems To Perform* is full of both.

Yellow butter, purple jelly, red jam, black bread.
Spread it thick,
Say it quick,
Yellow butter, purple jelly, red jam, black bread.
Spread it thicker,
Say it quicker,
Yellow butter, purple jelly, red jam, black bread.
Now repeat it,
While you eat it,
Yellow butter, purple jelly, red jam, black bread.
Don't talk
With your mouth full!

Mary Ann Hoberman, *Poems To Perform*

4 To learn to love language

Do you have a friend who can speak another language? Invite them over and persuade them to read aloud in their own tongue. It doesn't matter if it sounds like gobbledygook. Listen to the flow of the words and see if you can hear any patterns. Try reading something in a foreign language yourself. You are simply looking for the beauty of words and the sound they make.

SENSITIVE
SUBJECT

Do you get upset easily or find yourself worrying about things people have said to you, believing they're criticizing you? Are you often troubled by the belief that people are talking about you behind your back? If so, you could be a highly emotionally sensitive person. This may mean you experience situations with heightened senses and feelings, which isn't necessarily a bad thing—but sometimes it can result in you becoming overly worried because you read too much into situations. Read on to find out how to make your sensitivity work for you.

HOW TO MANAGE YOUR SENSITIVITY

1 Recognize you're highly sensitive
Accept that you're one of the many people who are naturally sensitive—it's a part of who you are. If you find yourself worrying about people talking about you behind your back or what someone said to you or how they said it, you should also remind yourself you could be feeling this way because you're sensitive and take a moment to consider whether you might be misinterpreting the situation.

2 Identify triggers
Consider what it is that tends to make you upset in these situations. Is it certain people, groups of friends, particular topics, if people discuss an aspect of your personality or make observations about your appearance? If you can identify a pattern, you can come up with a way of managing it, including being more prepared in these situations.

Ask yourself what exactly you're worrying about, what it is that's bothering you and consider whether you're overreacting. Do you need to stop being around the people who are upsetting you the most or to let people know how their comments affect you? It might be worth taking the time to ask a trusted friend if they think you're reading too much into a particular situation.

3 Building resilience
You may have heard the phrase about developing a "thick skin." This means being able to take insults, criticism, and unpleasantness without getting too emotional. It's about being calm and not breaking down when things aren't going well. Sometimes, a thick skin is a way of not letting situations affect you and your mental health. But it's about finding a balance and if someone is being cruel or bullying, report that behavior to someone you trust—and know that you're justified to feel upset.

4 Turn down the sensitivity
If someone makes comments about you that you find upsetting, you have choices. You could get upset and take their criticism or comments as the truth. Another option is to consider that this is just one person—possibly an unpleasant one if they're mocking you—and try not to let their comments affect you. If they're being cruel over an extended period of time and you feel they're bullying you, you should talk to someone about it—whether that's a trusted family member, a teacher, doctor, or the school nurse.

5 Learn to care only about what you think

It's important to understand that the only thing that truly matters is what you and your closest friends and family think. You may believe that a particular person is talking about you across the room—but if they are, so what? You can't change what they choose to think about you, but you can change how you react. Learn not to care about the actions of people who don't matter in your life.

6 Work out when to be silent

Practice letting comments go and not responding every time someone says something you find offensive or upsetting. It could be they're unaware of the effect of their words. If it's just small-minded people, or a comment not intended to be offensive, learn to let the words pass and forget them. It may be hard at first, but the more you practice, the more you will get into the habit.

7 Discover how to calm your mind

If you find you're doing exaggerated thinking, which means blowing things out of proportion or turning a small situation into a bigger one, try to remind yourself that this is precisely what you're doing—exaggerating. Be aware of this and it will help you to calm your thoughts. Recognize that you're someone who can easily feel overwhelmed, and try to schedule in daily downtime. Also be aware you may need to compromise—just because you don't like noise it doesn't mean everyone around you needs to be quiet. If other people's noise is bothering you, try moving into another room or go outside for a walk.

8 Learn when not to care about other people's opinions

Some of the happiest and most successful people have realized that worrying too much can be unhealthy and get in the way of achieving goals. It takes time, but learn to believe in yourself and not to seek others' approval, and trust you can make good decisions. If you care too much about others' opinions, you'll hold yourself back from being your true self and won't be comfortable in your skin. There are times to be sensitive, of course, but there are others when you can let go—enjoy your life without worrying about what others do or think.

NO PLACE TO HIDE

Everyone's had them. Those terrible embarrassing moments when you just want to sink through the floor. While you might not be able to stop your cheeks flushing red, there are ways to handle awkward situations

Have you ever been caught in an embarrassing situation? Those toe-curling moments that make you truly squirm? Maybe you waved to a stranger on your walk to school thinking it was a friend and everyone standing at the bus stop saw it happen. Or you weren't really concentrating in class and called your teacher "mom." When you're in the middle of an embarrassing moment, you'd rather be anywhere else. But try to remember that you're not alone—everyone has felt that way before. Here's some advice that might just help the next time you get toilet paper stuck on your shoe or you go sprawling across the school cafeteria…

1 You are allowed to get it wrong

Be open to the fact that you will make mistakes. It's okay to mess up. Nobody is perfect. Mistakes are a natural part of life, a learning experience that you need if you want to grow and move forward with greater confidence. Think back to times you witnessed someone else make a fool of themselves. How did you react? Did you help them to laugh it off, or did you try to make them feel bad about their mistake? Be your own best friend and let yourself off the hook.

2 Others might not pay much attention—or even care

The main reason people feel embarrassed is because others have noticed their mistake. But before you go off the deep end, take a good look around. Is anyone paying attention to you? Did they see what you did or hear what you said? If not, there's certainly no need to point it out.

3 Accept you're embarrassed

If it's clear, however, that all eyes are now firmly on you, don't panic. Accept that you're embarrassed and say so. There's nothing like owning up to a feeling to deflate its power over you. Plus it will be obvious to everyone around you how you're feeling, and if you point it out first, it takes the wind out of the sails of anyone about to say something mean. Some people may even do the kind thing and try to make you feel better.

4 Say you're sorry

Sometimes embarrassing blunders can happen at the worst of times. If your faux-pas has upset someone or caused a problem for others, make sure you take responsibility and apologize. But don't make it into a bigger deal than it already is. Explain why you think it happened and apologize once, genuinely.

5 But what if people keep going on about it?

People are more likely to forget what's happened if you don't make a big deal about it. It's as simple as that. If despite your best efforts some still don't want to let it go, try to laugh with them.

6 Take your mind off it

Don't allow this moment to ruin the rest of your day (or life!). Listen to music, go for a run, or watch some television—anything to stop you dwelling on it. Exercise is a great way to reduce the intensity of what you've experienced and will put things into perspective.

USE YOUR INTUITION

Tune in to your gut feelings to improve your life

Have you ever had a feeling about something and it turned out you were right? It could be you just knew which way to turn when going somewhere, maybe you had an inkling about which person to trust or who would be the one to win something in a competition?

Intuition is difficult to define but basically it means a gut feeling or instinct that has no logical reason. It's knowing something without understanding how or why you know it.

Some people refer to it as a hunch, a sixth sense, or unconscious knowledge— but there's a lot more to it than superstition. Researchers have discovered it's not something people are born with and doesn't just come naturally. It is a skill you can learn and, with practice, develop.

Read these tips on how to harness your intuition and use it to benefit your everyday life:

1 Body awareness
To learn to harness your intuition, you need to be aware of your body and how it feels throughout the day when it's relaxed, stressed, or happy. Take time to feel the air filling your lungs, feel your chest rise and fall, be aware of where any tension exists in your muscles, and how you feel throughout. When making decisions, any change in heart rate, sudden sweating, a sense of nervousness, or a feeling of dread in your chest or stomach could indicate a wrong choice or something negative, while a tingling feeling could mean the opposite.

2 Gut feelings
It's called a "gut" feeling for a reason. Often, when people are nervous or excited it's the butterflies-in-the-stomach feeling that is the most overwhelming sensation. Emotion surges one way or another when decision-making so learn to feel which is a positive feeling, which is nerves, excitement, or dread. The best way to listen to your stomach is to go somewhere you can be quiet and still and assess what exactly it is you are feeling and what your intuition is telling you.

3 Meditation moments

Take regular time out to meditate and slow down your racing mind so you can be more aware of your thoughts and become an expert in your own instincts. Remove yourself from the hustle and bustle of life, turn off any phones or electrical items which distract your brain, and sit somewhere quiet. Close your eyes and take slow, deep breaths, again taking time to consider the decision you are making. As you breathe, tune in to your feelings, thinking how your mind and body feel.

4 Guessing games

Guessing games are a great way to test your intuition and also improve your own instinctive skills. There are lots of things you can try. Guess who's on the other end of the phone when it rings without looking at the caller ID. When you watch TV or a movie, try to work out what happens next or what the ending might be. With friends, flip a coin and see how good you are at guessing which side it lands on. Predict who will score next in a game or what car color will drive past next. Making using your intuition fun is a great way to practice this skill. You can also discover just how good your intuition is.

5 Hunches

When you've got used to listening to your body and how it feels in certain situations and with different people, start using your intuition more often for bigger decisions. Consult it on what to wear, what to buy, or where to go. Pay attention to how it feels when your intuition was right and your decision was a good one. Use it around others so you get a sense of how you feel when you're with people you like. It's about recognizing how your body feels in moments and then being aware of these feelings in future. It's important you also know what happens when you make a bad decision, so you can work out what to steer clear of in future.

6 Trust yourself

The more you use your intuition, the easier it should be to trust your instincts and follow your inner guidance. In life, you will get many people advising you or telling you what to do. Sometimes it will make sense to follow their advice, but there will also be times when you have to make the decision and know what's right for you. Learn to trust your inner wisdom and follow your own path, learning from your good decisions and mistakes along the way.

ROOM TO
BREATHE

Everyone has moments when they need their own space.
Next time you want to slow down your racing thoughts, give
this exercise a try

* Find a quiet, comfortable place where you can sit for two minutes
  without distractions. Relax your shoulders and rest your hands on
  your thighs. Close your eyes and focus on your breathing.

* Notice parts of your body that feel tense: Your jaw? Your back and
  shoulders? Each time you take a breath in, see the air filling these
  places and watch as the tension drifts away with each breath out.

* Relax as you breathe. Imagine the thoughts racing around your
  mind and see them for what they are—fleeting and temporary.
  As you continue to breathe in and out, watch as the thoughts
  slowly float away from you.

* Place one hand on your chest and one on your stomach. Breathe in
  deeply through your nose for the count of four. As you breathe in
  your belly should swell. Hold the breath briefly, then blow the air out
  through your mouth for another count of four, feeling your hand fall
  with your belly. Repeat three more times, then open your eyes.

* Now that your thoughts have calmed, you can go on with your day.

DECISION TIME

Sometimes making decisions can be hard. Saying "yes" to one thing often means saying "no" to another. If you're having trouble making up your mind, here are some tips to follow...

How often do you hear people telling you to make good choices? For some people making a decision can be tricky. They freeze, like a deer in the headlights, because they're afraid of choosing the wrong thing. For others, decisions are made in double-quick time, but not thinking them through might mean they change their minds afterward, and then the same decision will have to be made again later.

Whenever you have more than one option, it's possible you could have made a "better" or "worse" choice. You might be able to guess where each decision will take you, but often you won't know for sure until time has passed.

There are some decisions, like what to wear or which shampoo to buy, that don't require too much thought because the consequences aren't so important (not usually, anyway!). More difficult ones, like which school or college to go to, who to choose as a friend, what type of friend you want to be, or how you should respond if you see someone who might need help, require more consideration.

Try to remember that no one is born with the ability to make a good decision—the more choices you make, the better you get at it, and often there is no right or wrong answer.

SIX STEPS TO EFFECTIVE DECISION MAKING

1 What is the problem?
Write down the decision you want to make. It's important you are clear on what it is you are trying to determine.

2 What is important to you?
Think about why you need to resolve this issue. This will give you an idea of how much it matters and how important it is for you to get it right. Ask yourself how your decision will affect you as a person and those you care about. Any decision you make should feel right—it needs to sit well with your personal values (the ideas you hold about what is important and what is not, what is wrong and what is right) and goals you want to achieve.

3 Do some research and ask advice
Don't feel you have to make tough decisions on your own. Speak to a friend or family member, they may have some sound advice and often just talking about your concerns can help. Doing some research can also be useful. Learning all you can about a project, option, or area allows you to make an informed choice and means you're less likely to find yourself saying: "If only I'd known that," later down the line.

4 List the possible options and alternatives
Make a list of every possible option you can choose from, even those that may sound silly at first. Put lots of ideas down on paper. Don't judge what you've written, just keep going until you can't think of any more.

5 What are the consequences?
Now that you have more information and a list of possible options, you can weigh up the pros and cons of each. For each one, ask yourself what the likely results would be of that decision. How will it affect you now? And in the future? Is it kind? Is it fair? Will it create a problem for someone else? Use all the information you've gathered so far and cross off any alternatives that simply won't work.

6 Decide on the best choice for you
Now for the scary part. It's time to choose. Remember, whatever decision you make, it's important to accept responsibility for the outcome. No one makes the right choices all the time, but you need to be prepared to stand by them, even when they don't work out. Good luck!

FIRST CRUSH

All you need to know about that intense feeling of infatuation

If you'd like to see your parents blush or giggle with embarrassment, ask them about their first crush. They'll probably go all misty-eyed as they tell you about the spindly teen, the cute boy or girl at school, or the lead singer in a long-gone band who first set their heart aflutter. First crushes can be inappropriate and baffling, but they're also entirely normal.

Infatuations are a crucial milestone on the uneven path to growing up—a sign that your emotions are maturing, just as your body is. Psychologist Carl E. Pickhardt, an expert on parenting and adolescence, says that although crushes are generally associated with finding someone physically attractive, there are three distinct types of infatuation, with each one giving a different insight into the person you are becoming.

You may develop an "identity" or role-model crush, for example, on someone of the same or opposite sex, of the same age or older, whom you admire. This will help you identify qualities and abilities you value in people, and which you would perhaps like to have. Or you may experience a "romantic" crush on someone you are attracted to, which acts as a prelude to recognizing who you'll want to date when you're older, or a "celebrity" crush on your favorite singer, actor, or vlogger.

Putting on a pedestal

Whatever your crush, though, you'll probably experience new sensations that, while exciting, may be difficult to handle. Chances are you'll get butterflies in your tummy and become tongue-tied whenever they're within earshot, and will long to be noticed by him or her, or even to dress, speak, and be like them.

When you have a crush on someone, you often don't see the person as they really are. You may project all sorts of abilities onto them, seeing them as the best-looking, cleverest, most athletic, artistic, musical being on the planet.

You may also find yourself drawing love hearts around your crush's name, or daydreaming about him or her, and that's fine as long as your infatuation doesn't become a fixation that takes over your life, makes you feel sad, leads you to do things you're not comfortable with, or to behave inappropriately.

It may help to think of a crush as a dress rehearsal that enables you to experience and try out emotions that you'll need later, when you're old enough to date. Sadly this may mean your heart will feel broken, but soon you'll bounce back and may even look at the object of your infatuation and wonder what all the fuss was about.

HEAD OVER HEELS

Your first crush can change your world. Here's what to remember:

1 What is a crush?
Simply put, a crush is a shift in feelings from liking someone to something more. Not love, but an infatuation, and it can be directed toward someone your own age or older, someone of the opposite or same sex, someone you know well, a little (the sibling of your best friend, say), or not at all (a celebrity or vlogger).

2 How to behave
A crush is sometimes called "puppy love" for a reason—namely because it leaves you skittish with excitement. In this heightened state of emotional upheaval, you might be tempted to run around telling everyone about your infatuation, but be warned—a person with a crush is an easy target for teasing. If you don't want you or your crush to be the brunt of classroom chat or social media gossip, keep your feelings to yourself. Likewise don't tease your friends if they tell you they like someone, and respect the feelings of anyone who has a crush on you regardless of whether you like them in the same way.

3 What to expect
Know that your first crush is unlikely to develop. Most often it remains a fantasy, an unrequited jumble of feelings that acts as a stepping stone toward your future self. It doesn't make it or those emotions any less real. While you're in the throes of puppy love, you may experience intense turmoil and sadness. This should pass quickly, but if it doesn't, think about speaking to a trusted adult, such as a family member, so they can support and look after you. If you find that too embarrassing, the school counselor or nurse may be able to talk through concerns you have about emotional feelings.

OPEN DOORS

Moving house and going to a new part of the country can be one of the most exciting times in your life—but it can also be one of the most challenging. Here are a few pointers to turn this potentially stressful situation into an exciting opportunity...

When you move you might have to change schools and leave behind close friends as well as a home full of memories. While your parents are sorting out the dull chores of arranging moving trucks and ordering boxes, there are many ways you can make the experience a positive one and memorable for all the right reasons.

1 When you don't want to move

Moving home can be hugely emotional. If it's been triggered by a difficult change of circumstance, or you are really happy at your current home and school, it can make the change even more challenging. If you're feeling sad or angry about what's happening, try to explore your parents' point of view as to why the family's moving. Talk to them about it rather than bottling it up as they will want to make sure you're happy. If you can't speak to them, chat to another relative or teacher. Try to accept the move will happen however you feel and see it as an opportunity to meet new friends and experience exciting things.

2 Pack it in

You're going to have pack all your belongings so you'll need to be super organized. Get a pen and paper and plan which items belong in each box. Remember to label the boxes, either with numbers or a word, so that its contents are clearly indicated. For example, you could have separate boxes for school work, photographs, clothes, and toiletries and cosmetics. Try to keep similar items together and write down what you're putting into each box. You'll be grateful for this boring-to-write list later on when you get to the new place and wonder where on earth your favorite shirt might be or where you put your journal. It's also a good idea to have an essentials box (see overleaf) in case you're too tired to unpack when you get to the new place.

3 Protect your things

Your parents will probably have lots of bubble wrap and paper to ensure fragile possessions are kept safe. Make sure you use it. You might think your expensive gadgets will be safe sitting loose in a box but they'll likely get thrown around quite a bit in the move. It's also handy not to leave all your packing until the last minute as that way you'll have time to think about which items need extra protection.

4 Sort it out

Moving home is the ideal time to go through all the things you've hoarded. Work out what you want to keep hold of and recycle, gift, or trash the rest. If you have clothes you've not worn for a while or books you no longer want, think about donating them to a charity—it'll free up space and you'll be doing something positive.

5 Keep a personal box with you

Make sure that you keep at hand important items such as phones, chargers, glasses or contact lenses, toiletries, makeup, tissues, or medicine you will need to find quickly. Perhaps put it in a brightly colored box or bag so you can find it easily if needed. Don't forget your toothbrush! Perhaps make yourself—and other members of your family if you're feeling generous—a "moving-day survivor kit" with things to help make the day easier, such as pens, notepaper, water, a candy bar or snacks, and perhaps something to ease the aches and pains of all the lifting. A nice bubble bath, maybe?

6 Saying goodbye

Luckily, with social media you'll still be able to keep in regular contact with your friends, though this won't help you feel less sad about leaving them and your school. To make it easier, plan a date for you to come back to visit them or for them to visit you. Moving homes and schools is part of life and people will come and go as you get older and start work or college. If your friends are good friends, they'll remain so despite the distance between you.

7 Do some research

Use the internet to find out about the area you're moving to and see if there are clubs you can join. Think about walking or running routes you can explore when you get there. If you can, spend a day at your new school ahead of the move—that way, you might get to know people your age before the big moving day and it will remove some of the anxiety of the first day at a new school.

8 Saying hello

When you arrive at your new home, spend time making your bedroom feel like it's truly yours. It can be exciting having a blank canvas on which to put your personal stamp—decide where your bed should go and where to hang pictures and place shelves. It can help make you feel at home.

A change of
COMPLEXION

Acne can strip confidence and wreak emotional havoc, but you don't have to stay silent if you're struggling to cope. Read on to discover simple ways to check in with your feelings if your skin breaks out

If you could watch the changes your body goes through as you morph from child to adolescent to young adult in fast motion, you would be amazed. The transformation that happens as your future self emerges from your preteen frame is nothing short of miraculous.

All these changes are the effects of nature taking its course, but the trouble is, that can sometimes play havoc with your appearance. Your hormones, which are responsible for you growing upward and outward, may throw you a curve ball, one that can be difficult to handle.

Take your skin. You've probably not given it a second thought before. But then you hit your teens and your flawless face becomes greasy and pimply as your oil (or sebaceous) glands go into overdrive, producing excess sebum.

Think positive
Ordinarily, sebum is your friend. It's the oily substance that keeps your hair shiny and your skin supple, but when there's too much of it, it can clog your pores, trapping bacteria and resulting in the dreaded assortment of pimples, whiteheads, and blackheads collectively known as acne. In its most severe form, acne can also appear on your back and chest and be both painful and emotionally devastating.

Even a mild form can leave you cowering in your room, too self-conscious to go out, and that's understandable. Your face is always on show. It's what people look at when they speak to you, so of course you want to have a blemish-free, "selfie-ready" complexion. The thing to remember is that your appearance is one tiny part of who you are. Your true self is your spirit and your qualities as a human being.

Try to focus on the fact that you are a wonderful friend, a loving son or daughter, and someone who is kind and thoughtful. If you do feel stressed, ask yourself this question: "Are these thoughts helping me?" If the answer's no, try to give yourself something else to think about—maybe phone a friend—until the moment passes.

It runs in the family

It may also help you to know that skin conditions are no obstacle to achieving your goals. Look at Rihanna and Lorde, both of whom are open about their pimples. Lorde's message that "flaws are okay" is absolutely right, while Rihanna has this tip: "When my skin has had it, I overdo the water. And I wear lipstick—it draws attention away from any blemishes." If lipstick also feels right for you, that's fine. But it isn't necessary—the natural you is fabulous, so go with whatever suits your style and personality.

Dr. Chris Bower, a consultant dermatologist (aka a skin specialist), deals in facts and says young people with pimples are the "normal" ones: "The vast majority of teenagers—80 percent—will get acne to some degree. Those who retain their flawless skin throughout their teens are in the minority." He describes acne as a cake made up of different layers. One layer is hormones, another tier is bacteria, another sebum, and a huge layer, about 50 percent, is genetic and is what you inherit. "If your parents had acne, then it's highly likely you'll also develop it," says Dr. Bower.

Knowing your mom and dad may have experienced what you're going through now, and come out the other side, may help, but it's still important to tell them, or another trusted adult, if you're struggling to cope.

Sadly, bullying and acne often go hand in hand. A study by the British Skin Foundation found that 62 percent of the 2,000 adolescents who took part in the survey had been called names. If you're being picked on at school or on social media, try to let your classmates know how awful they're making you feel but don't be afraid to ask an adult to help. Bullies are the ones with the problem, not you.

Finally, psychologists acknowledge that even mild breakouts can lead to depression and anxiety, while severe cases can cause enormous emotional problems. If you're withdrawing from friends, feeling low day after day, and letting your skin problems get in the way of you following your regular routine, then it's important to visit your doctor.

Acne is not something that should be trivialized. Far from being skin deep, its impact can be profound and long-lasting, but the good news is that it can be treated effectively—with ointments and tablets that are only available on prescription. You really don't have to live with it or suffer in silence. And, if you can, always remember that it doesn't define who you are—only you can define you.

ACTING ON ACNE

Dermatologists Dr. Chris Bower and Dr. Anjali Mahto have the following advice for anyone suffering with skin breakouts:

* Don't pick. Squeezing your pimples is the worst thing you can do.

* Keep your skin clean, but don't wash it more than twice a day or scrub it. Use a nonoily soap or a mild cleanser. If you have acne on your back, wash gently with an antibacterial soap and a brush.

* There is no evidence to link diet to bad skin. That said, fruit, vegetables, and water are always good for you.

* Wash your hair regularly and keep it off your face so that it doesn't irritate your cheeks or forehead.

* If you want to wear makeup, choose oil-free, water-based products that are noncomedogenic and nonacnegenic. Remove every last scrap of makeup before bed.

* Exercise regularly. It may not clear your acne, but it can improve your mood.

* Get effective treatment. If your breakouts are severe, see a doctor. They may recommend some prescription medication or refer you to a dermatologist. Medication can take a few weeks to work so don't give up on it if you don't see immediate results.

* Treating acne now can also prevent acne from worsening. Without treatment, acne sometimes becomes severe. When severe acne clears, it can leave permanent scars.

THE NATURAL LOOK

Feeling under pressure to follow the latest makeup trends? Maybe it's time to ditch the cosmetics and let your inner beauty shine...

Beauty trends come and go just like fashion, but it's worth remembering that the natural look is always on trend, especially when you're blessed with youthful good looks. You might not realize it, but your skin is softer and more supple now than it will be at any other stage of your life. Don't focus on the odd pimple or blemish because young skin has a natural, healthy glow that is always attractive and your eyes and lips have the vibrant color that makeup is designed to replace.

Some people wear makeup to boost their confidence, others use it as a mask to hide behind but for many, of course, makeup is a form of creative expression and a lot of fun. When you ditch the cosmetics and opt for the natural look, however, you are showing the world that you really are happy in your own skin.

So, before you reach for the fake lashes, take a moment to appreciate the looks you have at the moment. As you age, the skin becomes less elastic and is prone to wrinkles, which is why some older women apply foundation in an effort to replicate the youthful complexion they once had. As your skin doesn't need makeup at the moment, now is the time to make the most of your youthful beauty. Here's how...

TOP TIPS FOR A FRESH, CLEAN YOU

* Keep your skin looking lovely for longer by drinking plenty of water. This will flush out any toxins and impurities from your body.
* Eat healthily by making sure you get plenty of fresh fruit and vegetables into your daily diet. This will boost your immune system and make sure you feel well and your skin looks great.
* Moisturize your skin after washing with a simple lotion or cream that doesn't contain lots of chemicals as this will be kinder to your skin.
* Use natural lip balms instead of lipstick to keep your mouth clean and fresh.
* Don't overgroom your eyebrows as too much plucking or waxing can permanently damage their shape. Eyebrows help to frame the face so just brush them upward with an eyebrow brush.
* Instead of mascara, place a small amount of Vaseline™ on your finger and gently apply it to your eyelashes. This will keep them soft and curling upward whereas over time mascara will dry out your lashes and can cause them to break off.
* Keep your nails tidy by cleaning and cutting them regularly as this creates a good impression. While acrylics, gels, and enhancements can look dramatic, they're high-maintenance, expensive, and can cause damage to the underlying nail if not applied properly.
* Get plenty of sleep. Eight hours of uninterrupted sleep each night is the recommended amount.

WHY NATURAL BEAUTY IS BEST

Five reasons to forget the makeup and show your skin some natural love:

1 **Save money**
Opting for the natural look makes financial sense. Think of all the money you'll save by not splashing out on expensive eye shadows, mascaras, foundation, and eyeliners every few months (and that's to say nothing of the regular upkeep needed for artificial nails).

2 **Have a lie-in**
Enjoy a little extra time in bed in the mornings as you won't have to spend an hour in the bathroom carefully applying layers of makeup.

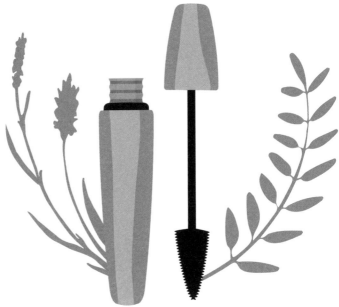

3 Help the environment

The more beauty products we buy, the more companies will produce, so do your bit for the environment by avoiding purchasing unnecessary products. Most makeup packaging is not biodegradable so when it's thrown out, it clogs up the Earth's landfill sites or ends up polluting the oceans.

4 Stay healthy

Applying makeup every day means you are more at risk of infections as tiny dirt particles that get into eye makeup can be transferred into your eyes. And remember, most makeup contains artificial ingredients, which isn't really what you want next to your skin all day. If you do sometimes wear makeup, remove it thoroughly in the evening. Also replace your mascara every six to eight weeks and sharpen your eye pencils regularly.

5 Party time

No one has to ditch the makeup bag completely, but why not keep it just for after school when you go out partying? Making a clear distinction between your daytime look and your play-time look will mean that getting ready to go out suddenly becomes a lot more fun.

HELP IS AT HAND

Whether you're stuck with homework or someone at school is saying mean things about you, you don't have to deal with things on your own

It can be scary to reach out for help, but there are plenty of things it's perfectly okay to need support with—in fact, anything that worries you is valid and you're allowed to talk about it if you want to. Seeking out what you need can actually take strength and determination, and it's one of many ways you can exercise self-care.

There are lots of people you can go to for advice, if you try your best to be open-minded and brave…

1 Friends
Friends are a fantastic support group, and you might even feel they know you better than your parents. If your friends live nearby, you might be able to escape to their house if things upset you at home. Never underestimate the power of friendship—even talking about your feelings with your friends can be help in itself.

2 Family
Your family wants the best for you, even if it might not feel that way sometimes. If they know you're worried about something, they can give you the best advice they've got. It's important to remember that even if you feel you can't talk openly with your parents, there might be another adult in your family you can trust.

3 Teachers
Everyone who works in your school has a duty to protect you. You might not think you connect with some of your teachers, but any member of staff can point you in the right direction and check in to see how you're doing—they can be an ally in a school where you might feel alone. Teachers can offer practical help, too, such as more support with studying for tests and homework. It's especially important to let someone at school know if you're being bullied—if you feel nervous about speaking to someone alone, ask a friend if they'll accompany you.

4 Online communities
Forums and blogs are a great way to find tips and tricks from other people going through the same things you are. Plenty of people discuss their thoughts about school and test stress, family problems, and bullying on YouTube™, and you'll find there are others who express similar experiences in the comments box.

5 Professional bodies
If you're overwhelmed by stress or worry, or you can't seem to find anything that cheers you up and the feeling won't go away, a doctor is open to you. They'll have advice on lifestyle, stress management, and can offer tips and advice on how to lift your mood. They can also refer you to a counselor—a trained professional who is there to talk and listen to you in a safe, private space—so that you can let out all your worries. Sometimes it's good to talk to somebody who doesn't know you and can give honest advice.

TIME TO GROW UP *(or is it?)*

The next chapter of your life is waiting to be written. There are exciting times ahead, but it takes courage to step out of your comfort zone

It's your time to shine. As you grow up you can start exploring your own identity, learn to discover the world by yourself and take your own decisions. But while you may be in a hurry to be independent, a part of you might also be worried about the changes, confusing feelings and difficult situations that could lie ahead. When you visualize your future, what do you see? A promising world full of opportunities, or a daunting life strewn with challenges?

Exciting and scary road
As you grow up you slowly step out of the comfort zone of childhood and gradually take control of your life. Not only is this process normal, it's necessary for you to eventually fly with your own wings.

Can you feel the desire to be free and different (and, at the same time, to belong and fit in)? It's an exciting—and scary—sensation.

It takes courage to move on from your 'old' life and step into the unknown. There is much to learn and there will be expectations on you—from society, parents, teachers and very often from yourself.

But remember it can also be fun if you allow yourself to enjoy the journey. You'll discover many new experiences, new feelings, new friends and a whole new world of possibilities.

If you don't feel ready, don't pressure yourself. You don't have to change overnight. Instead, you can slowly let go a little at a time while figuring out who you really are and what you want in life.

> *"Change is hard at first, messy in the middle, and gorgeous at the end"*

Robin Sharma

Starting point

If you feel confused and maybe anxious about what the future holds, you're not alone. Most people feel that same way. Even adults don't have answers to all the questions, but what's important is to try to use the knowledge and wisdom you gain over time.

It's experience, not time, that helps you better understand the world around you—and yourself. Experiences, whether they are good or bad, are precious and help you to gain emotional maturity and wisdom.

But what if you're worried about taking on the responsibilities that come with growing up? What if you want to stay young and carefree forever? It sounds appealing, but it might also be good to know about the person you can be and what you could achieve in life.

Fresh experiences

Consider growing up as a great adventure brimming with enriching experiences. There'll be crucial milestones that will give you confidence and reassurance about your future. And as you go through your teenage years, you'll naturally become more aware, more responsible and more capable.

Remember that being independent isn't the same as being on your own. There'll be people around to help, so don't be afraid to ask.

If you find yourself at odds with your parents or guardians, try to stay calm and talk to them honestly about any fears and frustrations you have (the school counselor or nurse can also help). This will help to build trust, which is a fundamental element of your future independence and all your relationships.

Growing up won't always be easy, but it will be worth it.

WAYS TO EMBRACE THE CHANGES

1 **You're not alone**
We all have to grow up, but you don't have to do it on your own. Ask for guidance. Guardians, older siblings, and friends will be happy, even honoured, to help you in such a personal matter. Make the most of the support you can get.

2 **Make decisions carefully**
Try not to throw yourself into dangerous situations, blindly follow others, or ignore the consequences of your actions. Approach each situation carefully to make decisions you're comfortable with and take time to appreciate what's happening in your life.

3 **No need to rush**
If you feel that things are not happening fast enough, stay patient. Things may not be as you expected right now, but give it time and don't be afraid to try again or do things differently. You have the power to make changes, and it's never too late to do so.

4 **Take a step back**
Sometimes life can be confusing and you might feel lost. Try not to get too emotional. Take a break and make a list of the different challenges you have to deal with. Address them one at a time, and cross them off as you move through, so you can appreciate your progress.

5 **Learn to be the best you**
Fear is not a nice feeling and can make you doubt your abilities. But don't let it stop you from realizing your potential. Be bold and try not to be afraid of growing up. Better, look forward to it and become the best person you can be.